Moving Home in Scotland: a guide to buying and selling your home

3rd edition
Derek Manson-Smith

May 2009
Edited by Sarah O'Neill

Crown Copyright 2009

First published November 1996
ISBN 9780114973506

Contents

Acknowledgements

I am grateful to Sarah O'Neill, Principal Policy Advocate and Solicitor at Consumer Focus Scotland, for her editorial guidance in revising the second edition of this book, which was previously published by the Scottish Consumer Council.

I would also like to thank the members of the conveyancing committee of the Law Society of Scotland, Scottish Government officials, Graeme Hartley of the Royal Incorporation of Chartered Surveyors in Scotland, Kennedy Foster of the Council of Mortgage Lenders, Alison Hatrick of the National Association of Estate Agents and David Thomas of the British Association of Removers for their comments on particular parts of this book.

Derek Manson-Smith
May 2009

About Consumer Focus Scotland

Consumer Focus Scotland started work in October 2008. Consumer Focus Scotland was formed through the merger of three organisations – the Scottish Consumer Council, energywatch Scotland, and Postwatch Scotland.

Consumer Focus Scotland works to secure a fair deal for consumers in both private markets and public services, by promoting fairer markets, greater value for money, and improved customer service. While producers of goods and services are usually well-organised and articulate when protecting their own interests, individual consumers very often are not. The people whose interests we represent are consumers of all kinds: they may be patients, tenants, parents, solicitors' clients, public transport users, or shoppers in a supermarket.

We have a commitment to work on behalf of vulnerable consumers, particularly in the energy and post sectors, and a duty to work on issues of sustainable development.

www.consumerfocus-scotland.org.uk

Part 1
Introduction

1.1. Why move?

Moving home can be a part of one of the more positive events of life, such as being able to afford a better home and standard of living or moving to another part of the country. Unfortunately, it is often associated with one of the more stressful events of life, such as changing job, starting a family, divorce, and bereavement.

This book will help to make moving home a less stressful experience for you. It describes the Scottish system of home purchase and sale, looks at the various choices you have, and gives guidance about the things to consider when making these choices. It also points out the pitfalls to be avoided at various stages in the process, and provides a checklist of things to remember leading up to the move. We hope it will help you to make the right move.

1.2. Do you really need to move?

Some people might consider the prospect of moving home to be so daunting that they may not want to move at all. It is worth considering whether you really need to move, especially if you are happy where you are. However, it may be that your home no longer suits you because your circumstances have changed since you moved there. Perhaps it is now too small or too big, or you or someone living with you has become disabled, or with increasing years can no longer cope with the layout. It may be that you could make some alterations to your home so that you don't have to move.

If you own your home and feel it is now too small, you could add an extension if you have a big enough garden to build on. If it is too big, it might be worth letting out a room or rooms, or sub-dividing it and selling or renting out a part of it. You might be able to borrow money from the lender who gave you your mortgage to make the alterations.

If your home needs serious repairs done to it, your local council may have a scheme of assistance for homeowners that will give you information and advice and may be able to give you a subsidised loan for the work – from 1 April 2010 all councils will have to have a scheme of assistance in place. If you or someone in your family is disabled and your home is short of basic necessities or needs adaptations to make it suitable to live in, you may be able to get a grant from your local council to cover installing the basic necessities or making the adaptations or both.

If you own your home and you or someone in your family is elderly and, because of this, cannot cope with the layout of your home, you could qualify for a grant to make suitable alterations if your council has a care-and-repair scheme.

However, if you don't want to or can't stay where you are, you may want to consider whether you want to rent or buy. Your answer may well depend on whether you are renting your home at the moment, or whether you own it. It is worth considering the advantages and disadvantages of both. While owning your own home has always been considered a worthwhile investment, the rate of increase in house prices seen in Scotland in the first half of the 2000s slowed and then decreased in the second half of the decade, although the market in Scotland has generally been more stable than that in England and Wales. Home ownership carries with it heavy responsibilities for maintenance of the property, and usually the burden of paying for a mortgage for many years in the future. Renting may be more flexible and better suited to those in more casual employment, or who tend to move from one part of the country to another, and it may be cheaper in the long run.

If you are getting older, you may wish to consider buying or renting some kind of sheltered accommodation. This book does not cover sheltered accommodation, but you can find details of where to go for more information about this subject at 1.3 below.

If you own your home and decide to move, you will need to decide whether it is best to buy a new home or sell your existing home first. This will depend on your circumstances and you should discuss them with your solicitor.

1.3. Further information

If you want to find out more about care-and-repair in your area, you should contact your local authority housing department. You can also contact the Care and Repair Forum Scotland, Suite 2.5, 135 Buchanan Street, Glasgow G1 2JA (tel: 0141 221 9879, e-mail: enquiries@careandrepairscotland.co.uk, http://www.careandrepairscotland.co.uk/)

Shelter Scotland, 4th floor, Scotiabank House, 6 South Charlotte Street, Edinburgh, EH2 4AW (tel: 0808 800 4444, http://scotland.shelter.org.uk/), provides information and advice for disabled people on buying a home, through its free advice line and on its website.

Ownership Options in Scotland, http://www.oois.org.uk, is a website that specialises in home ownership issues facing people with disabilities.

Buying retirement housing, Factsheet 2S, which includes sheltered accommodation, is available free of charge from Age Concern Scotland, Causewayside House, 160 Causewayside, Edinburg EH9 1PR (tel: 0845 125 97320, e-mail: enquiries@acscot.org.uk or download from http://www.ageconcernscotland.org.uk/helping_you/factsheets/8_buying-retirement-housing).

Part 2

What are you looking for?

2.1. What can you afford?

At the end of the day, it may be that cost is the deciding factor in whether you rent a furnished home, rent an unfurnished home or buy a home. The decision is yours but if you decide to buy, you should consider the essential costs that should be included in your budget, some of which you would of course still have to pay if you were renting.

You can use this table to help you work out the essential costs.

Table 2.1. Costs of buying and owning a home

One-off costs	£
Deposit towards purchase price	
Mortgage arrangement fee	
Mortgage indemnity guarantee (high lending fee)[1]	
Solicitor's fees and expenses	
Stamp duty land tax [2]	
Registration fees	
Removal	
Furniture etc	
Telephone or cable reconnection	
Total	

[1] Depending on the lender, this may be required if you are borrowing more than 75 per cent to 90 per cent of the purchase price

[2] Where the purchase price is more than £175,000 up to 31 December 2009 (see 5.8) on new housing developments.

Continuing costs	£
Property management or common charges [3]	
Land management fees [4]	
Mortgage payments/life insurance premiums	
Mortgage payment protection insurance	
Buildings insurance premiums	
Contents insurance premiums	
Exterior repairs and maintenance costs	
Interior repairs and maintenance costs	
Electricity bills	
Gas bills	
Telephone bills	
Internet/broadband/cable bills	
Council tax, water and sewerage charges	
Total	

[3] If you live in a block of flats or tenement

[4] While open spaces on housing developments have traditionally been owned and maintained by local authorities, in recent years new arrangements have emerged where private sector companies are involved in land management on new housing developments

2.2. Where do you want to live?

There is a combination of factors that could affect where you want to live.

- City, town or countryside? There are advantages and disadvantages to each. A city or town offers more choice of housing, services and social life. On the other hand, compared with the countryside, your environment may be more polluted and crowded, home prices and insurance rates may be higher, and services and public transport may be poor in some parts of cities. You can also feel isolated and lonely in a city. The countryside may offer a better environment, more possibilities for a garden or land, lower insurance costs and an easier pace of life. On the other hand, compared with city or town life, the countryside can be cut off in winter, there is less choice of housing, and services, leisure facilities and public transport may be poor or non-existent. You also have less choice of social activities and it may take a while to become accepted into the local community. If you work in a town or city and want to live in the countryside, you should think about how much time you want to spend commuting.

- Do you need to live close to where you work? If not, you will have a wider choice of neighbourhoods.

- Do you have children? Schools and access to leisure activities are an important consideration if you have children of school age.

- Do you have your own transport? If you are dependent on public transport, you will want to know that services are available and reliable.

2.3. What type of home do you want?

This will depend largely on what you can afford to buy. Within your budget, you should consider:

- The space you want. Are large rooms important, or the number of them? Do you want a garden and, if so, do you want one that needs lots of upkeep?

- Whether you want to live on one level or at ground level or both. A bungalow or ground-floor flat may be more appropriate for you if you are elderly or have a disability. If you don't mind living at the top of a tenement now, how will you feel if you later have young children or when you get older?

- How long you would expect to live in this home, the area or part of the country.

- How your circumstances might change in the future; for example, if you have children you may want more space.

2.4. New or old?

If you decide to buy a home, and depending on where you want to live, you have a choice of buying a newly-built or newly-converted home from a builder or developer or one that has been lived in. A new home has the advantages that:

• you are literally making a new start;

• it may be easier to get a mortgage;

• you are not dependent on someone else selling their home;

• the builder may be prepared to make some changes to suit you before it is finished;

• you can choose your own decoration;

• the price you pay may include extras, such as new carpets, curtains, a fitted kitchen and appliances;

• the property will carry a structural warranty or guarantee if the builder in registered with the National House-Building Council (NHBC), Zurich Insurance or Premier Guarantee (see 5.4.1);

• the builder may offer to take your current home in part exchange;

• the builder may offer a shared equity arrangement, which may make it easier for you to buy. For example, if a home costs £200,000 and the builder retains a 20 per cent share, you would pay £160,000. If you later sold it for £250,000, you would get £200,000 and the builder would get £50,000;

• if you are a first-time buyer on a low income, you may be able to buy under the Scottish Government's Low-cost Initiative for First-Time Buyers (LIFT) (see 3.3).

The disadvantages are:

• you may not have a choice as to when the home will be ready for you to move in, especially if you buy 'off-plan', and the eventual date of entry may be more geared to what suits the builder than you;

- if planning permission for an 'off-plan' home is granted, the builder may vary the layout of the estate from the plan shown to you when you bought the home, for example by substituting a different type of house or flats;

- there may be teething problems ('snagging') while the building settles in;

- you may have to spend time and money fitting and equipping it;

- you may have to do a lot of work to turn a building site into a garden;

- you may have to make stage payments (see 4.4) as the home is built and so end up borrowing to pay for two homes at the same time (see 5.6);

- you may be responsible for the costs of maintaining common land on a new development;

- extras, such as a cooker and fridge freezer, may be included in the price of the property when you buy it. If you decide to sell your home within a short time of buying it, the valuation will not include the value of these extras, which might mean that you get less than you paid for the home.

Buying a home that has been lived in will avoid these disadvantages. If it is less than 10-years old, it should still be covered by an NHBC warranty or a Premier Guarantee or if less than 15-years old by a Zurich Insurance warranty, if it was built by a builder registered under one of these schemes. The advantages of buying an older home are that:

- you will be moving into an established neighbourhood;

- you are more likely to have amenities such as shops, schools and public transport.

A disadvantage of an older home is that the upkeep costs of decoration, repairs and maintenance are likely to be higher than with a new home.

In the end, however, the decision on whether to buy new or old is often simply a matter of personal taste.

2.5. Living and storage space

Your home is not just for sleeping and eating in. Everyone will need their own space, and over time, the needs of your family will change. The needs of a three-year old are different from those of an eight-year old or a thirteen-year old.

The way your home is divided up can help you live the way you want or make living together difficult. An open–plan living area can make a small home appear more spacious, but it does not provide much privacy. Separate dining and living rooms can compensate for a lack of space in bedrooms to study or relax in. But this could mean that the rooms are quite small and it could be difficult to arrange furniture.

You should consider what you will need to store and where you will store it. As well as built-in storage, you will need space for free-standing furniture, shelving and coat racks and you will want the storage space to be in the right place. Where would you store the following?

baby buggy or pram	crockery	papers, bottles and other materials for recycling
bed linen	dirty laundry	
bicycles	DIY tools and supplies	pet food and cat litter
books	fresh food	pots and pans
boots and shoes	frozen food	sewing machine
broom	garden tools	sports equipment
bulk-buy items	hobby equipment	suitcases
CDs and DVDs	ironing board	tinned food
cleaning materials	kitchen refuse	toys
clothes	ladder/stepladder	umbrellas
coal or wood for an open fire	outdoor clothes	vacuum cleaner

Part 3

Buying a home: making a decision

3.1. Introduction

Scotland has its own legal system and law governing the ownership of land and property. Residential property is sold on the basis that the buyer gains the right to occupy and use it for as long as they own it. The concepts of leasehold and freehold found elsewhere in the United Kingdom do not generally apply in Scotland.

In Scotland, you make a written offer to buy and the seller accepts it in writing. A number of letters, known as 'missives', clarifying details and conditions of the offer and acceptance may be exchanged. Once these details are agreed, 'missives are concluded' and you have a binding contract (see 4.2). Should you be unable to fulfil your obligations in the missives, you may be liable for damages to the seller for resale costs and other losses incurred, which could amount to thousands of pounds. Therefore, before making an offer, you must get legal advice and arrange the finance to meet the purchase price (see 5.2).

Until missives are concluded, it is possible for either the buyer or seller to withdraw without penalty, although in practice this does not often happen. With the aim of speeding up the concluding of missives, in most parts of the country, solicitors have introduced a standard form of offer with conditions. Use of these significantly cuts down the time require to negotiate which can arise with 'non-standard' offers. You should check whether your solicitor uses the local standard offer.

Once the missives are concluded, however, you will have a binding contract and an agreed date of entry (see 4.2), and you cannot be 'gazumped'.

This is different from the situation in England, Wales and Northern Ireland, where someone wishing to buy a home makes an offer to buy 'subject to contract', which is not binding on either party. If this is accepted, he or she then has to find the funds to pay the price and the solicitors or conveyancers for both sides will check the title and draw up formal contract documents. When the parties are satisfied, formal contracts of sale are exchanged. Until this point, either party can withdraw without penalty and the seller could accept a better offer from a different prospective buyer. This is known as 'gazumping'.

The legal aspects of buying a home are explained in more detail in Part 5.

3.2. Buying your rented home

If you are a Scottish secure tenant of a council (including a housing management cooperative), a housing association or other registered social landlord (that is registered with the Scottish Housing Regulator) or a water authority, you may have a legal right to buy your home at a discount. This does not include accommodation provided under a contract of employment, that is, tied housing, certain temporary lettings, and homeless accommodation.

If you are unsure about whether you currently have a right to buy, you should check with your landlord.

The main requirements are:

- you must normally have spent at least two or five years (depending on when your tenancy started) as a secure tenant immediately before making the application;

- the home you rent must be occupied by you as your only or main home.

You need not have lived in the same home or have had the same landlord all the time. For example, you can also count time spent as a tenant of certain other bodies, such as the armed forces, a water authority or the Forestry Commission, unless you have had a break between tenancies that was within your control.

If your tenancy agreement dates back to before 30 September 2002 and it allows you to exercise the right to buy, the old terms and conditions will continue to apply to the right to buy for as long as you remain in that tenancy. This is known as a 'preserved right to buy'. However, with some limited exceptions, if your tenancy started on or after 30 September 2002 then the new terms associated with the modernised right to buy will apply.

You cannot buy your home if:

- you do not have a Scottish secure tenancy;

- your tenancy for the property you rent from a social landlord started after 30 September 2002 and falls within an area that has been designated as a 'pressured area' (your local authority should be able to confirm whether your neighbourhood has been designated);

- you rent from a charitable housing association that normally would have obtained charitable status before 18 July 2001, unless you already had a right to buy as a tenant of the landlord before 30 September 2002;

- your landlord has fewer than 100 homes;

- your home has special features for elderly people;

- it is part of a group housing scheme for people with special needs where the tenants have special facilities for their use or they are provided with housing support services or both;

- it is required by an islands council for accommodation connected with education;

- your home forms part of a fully-mutual cooperative housing association;

- your home is earmarked for demolition and your landlord has obtained a consent to refuse to sell.

In addition, your landlord may refuse to sell if you have arrears of rent, council tax, water and sewerage charges, or other amounts owing as a result of your current or a previous tenancy, or if your landlord is in the process of evicting you because of your conduct.

Contacts for further information on buying your rented home are given at 3.14.

LIFT

The Scottish Government's Low-Cost Initiative for First-Time Buyers (LIFT) includes shared ownership, shared equity and rural home ownership grants.

Shared ownership

Some housing associations operate a shared-ownership scheme, where the home is owned jointly between the landlord and tenant. You buy a share in the home (25 per cent, 50 per cent or 75 per cent of the purchase price) and pay rent on the balance. You can buy additional 25 per cent shares once a year, so that you eventually own the home, or you can carry on renting.

Shared equity

If you are on a low to moderate income and cannot afford the price of a home, the shared equity schemes allow you to share a stake (normally between 60 per cent and 80 per cent) of the market value of a property, with the option for increasing it to 100 per cent later. There are two schemes:

• The New Supply Shared Equity Scheme, which mostly involves homes that are newly built by registered social landlords – normally a housing association or a housing cooperative.

• The Open Market Shared Equity Pilot scheme, which allows people to purchase homes that are on the open market, that is, the scheme is not restricted to homes that are newly built by registered social landlords. From March 2009 to March 2010, the scheme is available across the whole of Scotland. Its availability after March 2010 will be reviewed.

The schemes are similar to shared ownership (see above), except that you will own the property outright and do not have to pay rent on the balance. For further information, see 3.14.

Many private house builders offer their own shared equity schemes, which are not limited to buyers on low incomes. Contact your local developer for further details.

Rural home ownership grants

If you live and work in a rural area and are a first-time buyer or you are a pensioner, long-term sick or disabled and have a local family connection, and cannot afford to buy a home without assistance, you may qualify for a Rural Home Ownership Grant towards the cost of renovating or building a home. For further information, see 3.14.

The Croft House Grant Scheme

If you are a registered crofter and you are inadequately housed, you may be able to get a grant to help you with the costs of building a new croft house or of improving an existing croft house. The Crofters Commission administers the scheme. For further information, see 3.14.

Tenants' incentive schemes

If you are a tenant of a council or registered social landlord you may qualify for a grant towards the purchase of a home in the private sector. Some councils operate cash-incentive schemes that aim to free up council accommodation for re-letting to others in housing need while providing financial assistance to aspiring homeowners. To find out more about the scheme, contact your landlord.

3.4. Where to look for homes for sale

3.4.1. New homes

If you want to buy a new home, you should contact a builder directly or the builder's sales agent. They normally advertise in local newspapers, on television, on the internet, sometimes through solicitors, and in *Scotland's New Homebuyer*, which is a free quarterly publication available from building societies, solicitors' property centres, selected banks and estate agents and on the internet at http://www.snhb.co.uk/.

3.4.2. Older homes

If you want to buy an older home, there are four main sources of information.

Newspapers

Most homes for sale are advertised in local newspapers by estate agents, solicitors and private individuals. Daily papers, such as The Herald, The Scotsman and The Press and Journal, usually have a set day for property advertisements and some publish a weekly supplement.

Estate agents

Remember that the estate agent is working for the seller, not for you, the prospective purchaser. This is the case even if the agent offers to provide other services, such as to help you find a mortgage. It is a good idea to contact local estate agents in the area and give them details of the type of home you are looking for and the price range you can afford. You can get details of any homes they have on offer and get on their postal and e-mail lists for details of homes that come onto the market later. The larger agents publish details of properties throughout Scotland in free news-sheets and on their websites. An estate agent will usually arrange for you to view likely homes and, if you are interested, will negotiate with you on behalf of the seller. As with solicitors' property centres (see below), you can register with them on their websites for updates by e-mail.

Property websites

You can search for property and register for e-mail alerts on property websites, such as;

• Rightmove at http://www.rightmove.co.uk/property/ Scotland.html

• Property Window at http://www.propertywindow.com/

• Property Finder at http://www.propertyfinder.com/uk/property/ scotland

• s1 Homes at http://www.s1homes.com/directory/

Solicitors' property centres

Scottish solicitors have a long-standing tradition of selling property. Most are members of their local solicitors' property centres, which display properties being sold by solicitors who subscribe to them. You should contact local property centres and give them details of the type of home you are looking for and the price range you can afford. They keep details of properties on offer and maintain mailing lists for homes coming onto the market. The larger property centres publish free news-sheets that list all the properties offered for sale by their subscribing solicitors. If you register your requirements on their websites, you will be sent details of suitable properties by e-mail. You can find details of solicitors' property centres on the Scottish Solicitors Property Centres website at http://www.sspc.co.uk/. Usually, viewing will be arranged through the solicitor working for the seller, and the property details will include information on viewing. Any subsequent negotiations are conducted with the selling solicitor. Remember that, as is the case with an estate agent, the solicitor who is selling the property through a property centre is working for the seller, not you.

3.5. Property descriptions and information

It is important to gather all the information you can about any property you are interested in.

The Consumer Protection from Unfair Trading Regulations 2008 ban a wide range of practices, including: telling you that the price for a new house will be increased in seven days time, in order to pressurise you into making an immediate decision to buy; giving you materially inaccurate information on market conditions or on the possibility of finding a house, with the intention of inducing you to acquire it at conditions less favourable than normal market conditions.

The Property Misdescriptions Act 1991 makes it an offence for an estate agent, a builder or a solicitor to give any description of a property that is not truthful, such as advertising a house as having three bedrooms, when it only has two, or describing as a bedroom a third room that is too small to fit a bed in, although it does not make any rules on the topics covered or the amount of detail.

If you believe that you have been given any information that is misleading or untruthful, you can refer it to your local trading standards service, which has power to take action against the selling agent if necessary (see under the entry for your local council in the phone book). If a builder or agent is successfully prosecuted under the 1991 Act, you may be able to sue for damages.

New homes

Most builders provide useful information about new homes. If you plan to buy a new home, you should make sure that you get the following information:

- A leaflet with floor plans and dimensions: this will give you an idea of how the rooms are arranged.

- A plan of the site layout: this will give you an idea of the size of the site. It can also help you choose the location of a home on the site if it has not yet been built and may tell you something about parking and road safety.

- A specification sheet: this will describe the type of walls, doors, windows, kitchen and bathroom fittings.

- Information, preferably in writing, on when the house will be ready for occupation.

Older homes

Solicitors' property centres and estate agents do not normally provide plans but they usually provide a property description, and they must provide you with a Home Report (see 4.1) unless the home is newly-converted. If you are responding to an advertisement placed by a private seller, you may not get any written information describing the property but you must be given a Home Report. If you do receive any written information or a Home Report from a private seller, remember that it is not covered by the Property Misdescriptions Act. A property description will give you a general idea of the property, which should help you decide whether it is worth viewing. The dimensions given are usually only approximate so, if they are important to you, you should check them on site. It is important to check the description carefully to see what is included, such as cookers, carpets, curtains, and so on. If you later make an offer to buy, you should make sure that these items are specified in the offer by your solicitor.

3.6. Viewing

Before you view a home, you should think about the things that are important to you. The following list gives some suggestions:

- the neighbourhood – local amenities, such as schools, places of worship, shops and public transport, and neighbouring properties;

- car parking;

- space for children to play;

- gardens and balconies;

- safety and security;

- open-plan living space or separate rooms;

- fittings, fixtures and equipment – what you need that may be included and what you will be wanting to take with you;

- storage space;
- the layout of rooms;
- noise from neighbours;
- recycling facilities;
- daylight and views;
- heating costs;
- council tax band;
- broadband access, cable television connections or satellite dish;
- whether old lead piping has been replaced;
- alterations that have been done or that you may wish to do (see 3.7);
- in the case of flats, whether the building is managed by the owners or a property manager (sometimes known as a factor).

Draw up a checklist of things that are important to you. It will help you think methodically about your needs, remind you about things you may easily forget, and help you decide which features are most important.

When you view properties, keep a record of those you visit and make notes on the property description. Collect as much information as you can so that you can read through it later. Some of the above information, such as information about parking, alterations and property management arrangements, should be contained in the property questionnaire part of the home report (see 4.1.2)

If you are interested in a particular property, you should visit the neighbourhood and the home again during the day and at night, on a weekday and a weekend. They may seem very different at different times.

3.7. Alterations

3.7.1. Alterations made by the seller or previous owner

If the seller or a previous owner has made any alterations to a property you want to buy, these may have needed planning permission or building control consent or both. Some properties that have special character may also be listed as of special architectural or historic interest: changes to these buildings need listed building consent. There may also be conditions in the title deeds that prohibit alterations that have been made. The property questionnaire in the Home Report (see 4.1.2) will tell you:

- whether any alterations, additions or extensions have been carried out by the seller;
- whether any necessary permissions, consents, building warrants or certificates for the work were obtained; and
- if so, whether any guarantees were provided.

However, particularly if the seller has only owned the house for a short while, there may be earlier alterations. If you suspect this may be the case, you should ask your solicitor to look into this. If any permission, warrant, consent or certificate has not been obtained that should have been, you could be faced with very expensive work to meet the conditions or undo the work. If you are in any doubt, you may wish to instruct a building surveyor to check the position or ask your solicitor to seek warranties from the seller in the offer for the property.

3.7.2. Alterations you may want to make

If you are planning to make alterations to a property you are going to buy, you should find out whether you need, and can get, permission before you make an offer as this could affect your decision to buy.

It is very important to make sure that any planning consents, building warrants and completion certificates are placed with the title deeds for safekeeping, as you will need to provide these when you sell the property in the future.

Planning permission

You will not need planning permission for certain minor changes, for example, most loft conversions or dormer windows, hedges, low fences and walls, a satellite dish up to 90 cm in diameter, or for the installation of certain microgeneration equipment, such as solar panels, biomass systems and heat pumps. However, some loft conversions and dormer windows do require planning permission and the installation of microgeneration equipment is not permitted on the walls of buildings containing flats. For some changes, you do not need planning permission, provided certain conditions are fulfilled – these include, for example, small extensions, garages and outhouses. Most porches to the front of a property do require planning permission.

You will need permission or consent or both, even for those changes that do not normally require it, if:

- the property is a listed building (that is, a building listed under the Town and Country Planning (Scotland) Acts as being of special architectural or historic interest);

- the property is in a conservation area (that is, an area designated as of special architectural or historic interest, the character or appearance of which it is desirable to preserve or enhance);

- in other circumstances if conditions have been imposed, restricting the types of changes allowed.

It is important to be absolutely sure about the position, so you should always contact the planning department at your local council before starting any work.

Building control consent

As well as planning permission, you may need building control consent. This takes the form of a warrant (or permission) from the local council building control department certifying that the proposed building work complies with the building standards regulations. For example, you need to have building control approval for internal and external alterations to existing buildings, new or altered drainage systems and the installation of certain microgeneration equipment, such as solar panels, biomass systems and heat pumps. Again, you should check beforehand whether the work you are planning to do needs a building control warrant.

You do not need approval for minor work such as general repairs, the installation of fitted wardrobes or electric heaters, and the installation of gas appliances by approved fitters.

3.8. Special treatments, guarantees and insurance

The property questionnaire in the Home Report (see 4.1) should tell you about any special treatments that have been carried out in the property, such as treatment for wet or dry rot, or the installation of a damp-proof course.

Special treatments should be covered by a guarantee or insurance policy. Make sure that your solicitor checks that any guarantees or insurance policies are valid and can be transferred to you. If the company that provided the guarantee has gone out of business, then it will be useless unless it is backed by insurance. It will also be of little use if the guarantee period is due to run out soon.

If the single survey in the Home Report indicates the need for special treatments, you should ask for a full report, specification and quotation before you decide how much to offer. Most reputable preservation companies will give you a free quotation.

A home that was built, converted or renovated 10 years ago or less may be covered by a National House-Building Council Buildmark warranty or Premier Guarantee warranty and one that is less than 15 years old may be covered by a Zurich Building Guarantee warranty (see 5.4.1 and 5.4.2). These warranty policies can be transferred to a new owner but they exclude damage or defects that you knew about when you bought the home or which might reasonably have been discovered by the survey. If the survey shows up problems covered by a warranty policy, you should find out if the current owner is prepared to make a claim before you consider making an offer.

Again, you should keep any warranty policy documents with the title deeds.

3.9. Fixtures, appliances and central heating

Any fixtures and appliances included in the purchase price should be in reasonable working order. You should try to find out how old they are, whether they are still under guarantee and, if so, whether the guarantees can be transferred to you.

Central heating systems can cause problems. The property questionnaire in the Home Report (see 4.1) should tell you how old the system is, whether there is a maintenance contract, and when an engineer last looked at it. The surveyor who carried out the single survey should have checked if the system is working and appears adequate. But remember that the surveyor is not a heating engineer. For peace of mind you may wish to instruct a heating engineer to check the system, although the seller may not agree this. Normally, in the missives, the seller will provide at least a limited warranty, for example that the system will be in working order at the date of entry, although any claim would require to be made within a few days of settlement. Any other repairs or replacements could involve considerable expense and you may need to take these into account when deciding how much to offer for the property.

3.10. Running costs

You should find out as much as you can about the running costs of a home before you buy. Details of some of the outgoings should be easy to get. For example, information about the council tax banding will be available from the property questionnaire in the Home Report (see 4.1).

Energy costs are a major outgoing. For new homes, you should be provided with an energy performance certificate, which states the energy efficiency of a building based on the way the building is used and suggests ways in which its efficiency could be improved.

For homes that are not newly built, the Home Report will include an energy report, which includes a home's energy efficiency rating and advice and information about how to make a home more energy efficient and save fuel costs.

The following list includes the main outgoings you should allow for:

• Mortgage payments (see Part 6)

• Council tax, water and sewerage charges

• Insurance premiums – contents and buildings (see 3.11 and 3.13.5), mortgage payment protection (see 6.9), life (see 6.8)

• Fuel – electricity and gas, oil, or coal

• Telephone, internet and cable/satellite

• Television licence

• Repairs and redecoration – interior and exterior

• Property management or common charges (if you live in a flat – see 3.13)

• Land management fees that may be levied if you buy in a new housing development.

3.11. Insurance

3.11.1 Contents

You are under no obligation to insure the contents of your home. However, a home contents insurance policy, besides covering your belongings, provides valuable additional cover. If your home is badly damaged and you have to move out while repairs are carried out, the policy will usually pay towards the reasonable cost of alternative accommodation. The policy will also usually cover you for any legal liability for injury to someone or damage to his or her property while in your home, and it may also cover you for your legal liability in day-to-day life if, for example, as a pedestrian you cause an expensive traffic accident. It is important to shop around for insurance, to check what will be covered, and to read your policy once you receive it to see what is included.

3.11.2. Buildings

While it is strongly advisable, if you buy a detached or semi-detached house you do not have any legal obligation to insure it unless the title deeds require it. However, if you have a mortgage, the lender will insist that you take out buildings insurance covering the reinstatement cost of your home, that is, the full cost of rebuilding the property and not just its current market value. Where appropriate, it will include outbuilding and garages, demolition and site clearance and certain professional fees.

If you intend to buy a flat, see 3.13.5, which tells you about the responsibilities of flat owners to insure their property.

Mortgage lenders will insist that your property is protected by buildings insurance and most will offer buildings insurance as part of a package with the mortgage. However, you don't have to take what they offer and you should shop around for the best policy for your needs. If you buy your insurance elsewhere, your lender may make a small charge for checking that the policy is suitable backing for the loan.

You are responsible for making sure that your insurance cover is adequate. Any significant under-insurance could mean that any claim you make might be reduced or even rejected. The single survey, which is part of the Home Report (see 4.1), will contain a recommended amount for buildings insurance.

Buildings insurance, as well as covering the structure together with the fixtures and fittings, also covers your legal liability as the owner. For example, if someone is injured or damage is caused to their property because of your negligence, you could find yourself having to pay damages or compensation, which may amount to a lot of money.

If you live in a flat or share ground or property with other people, your insurance should cover your share of responsibility for common parts (see 3.13.4).

3.12. Potential problems with neighbourhoods and neighbours

3.12.1. The neighbourhood

You can get a good idea of a neighbourhood by visiting it at different times of the day and week before you buy. Consider things like vacant land nearby. This may become the site of a new housing or industrial development. How would this alter the neighbourhood and the view from your home? Other factors to consider are the proximity of things like a pub, a take-away, a school playground or a disco. Would you mind living near these? Are there recycling facilities in the neighbourhood within walking distance? The neighbourhood may be too noisy for you or there may be heavy traffic congestion or pollution at certain times of the day. Look out for potential problems such as factories and dairies, quarries, goods yards, railway lines and airports and decide whether these may affect you.

Car parking can cause problems, even if you do not own a car. The neighbourhood will be more pleasant to live in if there is adequate parking for residents and visitors. A shortage of parking spaces can lead to disputes between neighbours. In some inner-city areas, car owners have to pay for a resident's parking permit to park outside their homes.

3.12.2. Neighbours

You have to share your neighbourhood with people who may have very different lifestyles to yours. Good neighbours are invaluable, but unsociable neighbours can make life a nightmare. Although you cannot choose your neighbours, you can look for features that reduce the likelihood of problems. These include marked parking spaces for visitors' cars, separate driveways and front paths, doorways that do not face each other directly, and proper bin-storage areas.

If you live in a block of flats, the garden may belong to the ground floor flat or be shared with other owners. If it is shared and you live on the ground floor, you may have little control over who can use the garden. You may not enjoy a garden full of party-goers or children playing near your windows.

Noise is a major cause of disputes between neighbours. If you can hear your neighbours, they can also hear you. When you look at a home, you should consider:

• the quality of the construction of the home: for example, party walls between flats, terraced and semi-detached houses, and, in older converted houses, the floors between flats may not provide enough noise insulation;

• the layout, or the way spaces in neighbouring homes are organised: for example, the living room, kitchen, hall and bathroom of a flat on one floor should not lie over bedrooms in the flat below.

It is difficult to do anything about bad neighbours once you move in – except move. So, try to find out before you buy. Ask the seller what the neighbours are like (although if the neighbours are noisy, they are unlikely to tell you), whether they have children or pets, how long have they lived there, and so on.

3.12.3. Shared boundaries

Where you share a wall (be it part of a building or a boundary wall), fence or hedge that separates your property from another, you will probably have a joint responsibility for its maintenance. The title deeds may say what part is owned by whom and may specify the share of the maintenance.

3.13. Responsibilities of flat owners

Owning a flat is a lot more complicated than owning a house. When you own a house, you only have to look after your own property. When you buy a flat, you also take on a share with the other owners of maintaining the common parts of the building. These can include the roof, the shared entrance, the stairs, a lift (if there is one), the outside walls, the garden and, in some cases, cleaning and caretaking services.

3.13.1. Tenements and multiple-occupancy buildings

Legally, every flat owner has some responsibility towards the repair and maintenance of shared areas and services. This means that you also have to pay your share of the costs. In many cases, the title deeds of the property will set out the common areas of the building you can use and for which you are responsible, what share of the maintenance you pay, how decisions should be reached among the various owners, and whether you have to employ a property manager (sometimes known as a factor) to look after the property.

If you buy a new, modern or converted flat, there will usually be a deed of conditions about the development or the building. This sets out what you can and cannot do with your property, for example, whether you can keep pets or restrictions on the decoration of the outside of your property, and may provide for the appointment of a property manager.

If there are gaps in the title deeds, such as them not saying how decisions should be taken or not describing all the common parts, or defects, such as allocating shares of costs that do not add up to 100 per cent, then the Tenement Management Scheme will fill the gaps or correct the defects. The scheme does not affect your ownership of your flat. You can find further information in *Common Repair, Common Sense: a homeowner's guide to the management and maintenance of common property* (see 3.14).

3.13.2. Property managers

Many flats, especially in Glasgow and the West of Scotland, have a property manager to look after repairs and maintenance. This is common in old tenement buildings in Glasgow but is also popular in modern blocks of flats throughout Scotland. Property managers are firms that specialise in maintaining multiple-ownership properties. Property management firms will typically provide the following services: instructing contractors to carry out repairs; organising common property insurance cover; and the cleaning and maintenance of common areas. Property managers usually bill owners quarterly but some bill annually or every six months. A small number may be able to arrange for owners to pay monthly by direct debit. Owners are charged a service charge (sometimes called an administration fee) and for the cost of any maintenance or common repair costs. If large or expensive repairs are required, the property manager may insist on the approval of all the owners and ask for advance payment before the work is carried out.

You do not have to have a property manager even if it is required by the title deeds or deed of conditions. If the building already has a property manager, two-thirds of the owners can agree to dismiss the property manager, and arrange for maintenance and repairs as necessary. Similarly, provided a majority of the owners agree, you can appoint or change a property manager.

3.13.3. Former rented flats

If you decide to buy a flat that you have been renting from a public-sector body, such as a council or a registered social landlord (see 3.2), the same general rules apply as to any other flat buyer. The title deeds will set out your rights and duties towards other owners. However, your former landlord may own some of the other flats and, if it owns most of them, it will be open to it to do repairs and maintenance as and when it decides. As a joint owner, you will be responsible for meeting your share of the costs.

In addition to its role as an owner, the council or registered social landlord may also act as the property manager and organise repairs and maintenance. It will then bill you for your share according to your title deeds. Alternatively it may employ a private sector property manager to carry out this role. You should find out about the arrangements for property management before committing to buying a former council or housing association property.

You should be absolutely clear about what you are buying, for example, whether you actually own or share ownership of the garden or drying green, which will mean that you also have to share maintenance costs, or whether you only have rights of access.

3.13.4. Sheltered and retirement housing

Services in sheltered and retirement housing can include shared facilities, such as a lounge, laundry, guest bedrooms, an emergency alarm system or the services of a warden or both. Services include cleaning, maintenance and insurance of the common parts. You pay your share of the costs of amenities and services through a service charge. These charges can be particularly significant and will go up over the years, so it is important to find out as much as you can about them.

There is a Framework Code of Management Practice for Owner Occupied Sheltered Housing. For further information, see 3.14.

3.13.5. Insurance

Adequate insurance is a common property obligation. You are not adequately insured unless you and all your fellow owners in the building are adequately insured. While you are responsible for insuring your own flat, you and your fellow owners are legally obliged to insure your flats for their reinstatement values. When you take out a mortgage, your lender will insist that you have buildings insurance that meets its requirements (see 3.11.2). This should cover damage to your own flat and also your share of the common parts of the property. However, problems can arise if any other owners do not meet their common property obligations and are under-insured. In the event of a claim for repairs to the common parts of the building, the cover provided by those who are not adequately insured may not be enough to pay the costs. If one owner is not adequately insured, any of the other owners can enforce this obligation in the courts.

An alternative is a common insurance policy for the whole building, with each owner paying a share of the costs. Mortgage lenders will usually be willing to allow you to take out a share of a common policy rather than having your own insurance, provided the policy offers adequate cover. You will need to get a copy of the policy to show your lender.

If you buy a flat in a building that has a property manager, you will probably find that there is already a common insurance policy covering the whole building. The duty to have this is usually in the title deeds. The property manager collects each owner's share of the premiums and pays it to the insurance company. While you may object to having to pay towards a common policy, in many cases there is little you can do about it. Sometimes, the cover provided by a common policy has not been kept at an adequate level. This creates no problems if each owner has adequate cover but it can lead to problems if some owners are not adequately covered. If a common policy provided by a property manager does not cover the reinstatement value of the building, you and your fellow owners can instruct the property manager to arrange adequate cover.

3.14. Further information

Your right to buy your home. Available free of charge from the Scottish Government, Victoria Quay, Edinburgh EH6 6QQ (tel: 08457 741 741) or http://www.scotland.gov.uk/Resource/Doc/46951/0030452.pdf, council housing departments and citizens' advice bureaux (see the phone book).

Low-cost Initiative for First-Time Buyers (LIFT)

• New Supply Shared Equity Scheme. Available at a cost of £2.50 from Blackwell's Bookshop, 53 South Bridge, Edinburgh EH1 1YS (tel: 0131 622 8283 or 0131 622 8258, e-mail: business.edinburgh@blackwell.co.uk) or: http://www.scotland.gov.uk/Resource/Doc/235963/0064685.pdf or see http://www.scotland.gov.uk/lift for contact details for your local housing association.

• Open Market Shared Equity Pilot. Available free of charge from http://www.scotland.gov.uk/lift or by contacting your local housing association who administers the scheme in your area (see the website or call the Scottish Government on 08457 741 741 and ask to speak to your local Housing Investment Area Office for contact details).

• Rural Home Ownership Grants; helping you become a home owner in rural areas. Available free of charge from the Scottish Government, Victoria Quay, Edinburgh EH6 6QQ (tel: 08457 741 741) or http://www.communitiesscotland.gov.uk/stellent/ groups/public/documents/webpages/cs_016499.pdf

Croft House Grant Scheme. Contact Crofters Commission, The Business Centre (Unit 3), Crossapol, Isle of Tiree PA77 6UP (tel: 01879 220 240, e-mail: chgs@scotland.gsi.gov. uk, http://www.crofterscommission.org.uk/Scottish-House-Grant-Scheme-CHGS.asp)

Buying retirement housing. Factsheet 2S. Available free of charge from Age Concern Scotland, Causewayside House, 160 Causewayside, Edinburgh EH9 1PR (tel: 0845 125 97320, e-mail: enquiries@acscot.org.uk) or http://www. ageconcernscotland.org.uk/helping_you/factsheets/8_buying-retirement-housing

The following publications are available from the National House-Building Council Scotland, Suite 4, Pavilion 5, 5 New Mart Place, Edinburgh EH14 1RW (tel: 0844 633 1000, e-mail: cssupport@nhbc.co.uk, http://www.nhbc.co.uk):
NHBC – who we are, what we do...
Buying a New Home
A Guide to your New Home
NHBC Buildmark. Your warranty and insurance cover.
NHBC Customer Charter

Information on the Zurich Insurance Building Guarantee is available from Zurich Insurance Building Guarantee, Zurich House, 2 Gladiator Way, Farnborough, Hampshire GU14 0NL (tel: 01252 377474, e-mail: building.guarantee@uk.zurich.com, https://www.zurich.co.uk/buildingguarantee/homeowners/ introduction.htm)

Information on the Premier Guarantee is available from Premier Guarantee, Haymarket Court, Hinson Street, Birkenhead CH41 5BX (tel: 0151 650 4343, e-mail: info@premierguarantee. co.uk, http://www.premierguarantee.co.uk)

Common Repair, Common Sense: a homeowner's guide to the management and maintenance of common property, is available from is available from Consumer Focus Scotland, Royal Exchange House, 100 Queen Street, Glasgow G1 3DN (tel:01412265261,e-mail:mail@consumerfocus-scotland.org.uk, http://www.consumerfocus-scotland.org.uk)

A Framework Code of Management Practice for Owner Occupied Sheltered Housing http://www.scotland.gov.uk/library2/doc12/oosh-00.asp was published by the Scottish Executive in 2000. At the time of writing, the code was under review by the Scottish Government.

Part 4

The Home Report and surveys

4.1. The Home Report

With some exceptions (see 4.1.4), sellers must provide potential buyers with a copy of a Home Report. The report has three parts:

- A single survey and valuation
- A property questionnaire
- An energy report

4.1.1. The single survey and valuation

The single survey report tells potential buyers about the type, accommodation, neighbourhood, age and construction of the property, its condition inside and outside and the services and the common grounds. A condition category will be given for each of 24 separate elements of the property surveyed, for example, the accommodation, the windows, external doors and joinery, the roofing and the neighbourhood.

Category 1 – No immediate action or repair is needed.

Category 2 – Repairs or replacement requiring future attention, but potential purchasers are advised to get estimates.

Category 3 – Urgent repairs or replacements are needed now. Failure to deal with them may cause problems to other parts of the property or cause a safety hazard. Estimates for repairs or replacement are needed now.

The survey also tells potential buyers about accessibility, information that should be checked with a solicitor and gives an opinion of the property's market value (a valuation) and an estimated reinstatement cost for insurance purposes. However, until an offer is accepted, the buyer will not be able to discuss the report with the surveyor who prepared it and in some cases, particularly with older and more unusual property, potential buyers may wish to consider whether it may be advisable to instruct their own surveys.

In addition, surveyors will offer sellers a generic mortgage valuation report that puts the valuation information into the lender's standard format. It may be useful for the buyer in any discussions with lenders about a prospective purchase. While this is not a legal requirement for a Home Report, the seller is likely to choose to accept the offer as it will help the marketing of the property. If he or she decides not to accept the offer of a generic mortgage valuation report, or if the survey was carried out sometime ago, or the loan is high compared with the likely value of the property, it is possible that the lender will ask the potential buyer to pay for one. Potential buyers should also check that the valuation report is acceptable to their lenders.

Lenders usually have a list of chartered surveyor firms from which they will accept generic mortgage valuation reports. Therefore, buyers should ask their lenders as soon as possible if they will accept the generic mortgage valuation report provided by the seller.

4.1.2. The property questionnaire

The property questionnaire contains information for purchasers, much of which will also be useful for solicitors and surveyors. It includes:

• how long the seller has owned it;

• its council tax band;

• parking arrangements;

• whether it is listed or in a conservation area;

• issues that have affected the property, such as fire or storm damage that may have occurred in the past or the existence of asbestos;

- alterations, additions or extensions that have been made to the home;
- details of services;
- responsibilities for shared or common areas;
- charges associated with the property;
- details of specialist works and guarantees;
- boundaries;
- details of any notices that affect the property.

4.1.3. The energy report

The energy report, which is likely to be prepared by the surveyor who inspected the house, provides an energy efficiency rating for the house. It gives information on the cost of running the property in terms of heating, lighting and water heating and contact details for further advice and information about how to make a home more energy efficient and save fuel costs. It includes an Energy Performance Certificate, which gives information on the house's energy performance rating and its environmental impact in terms of carbon dioxide emissions (similar to that found on washing machines and other electrical appliances) on a scale from A to G, with A being the most energy efficient and environmentally friendly, and how cost-effect improvements can be made. The average rating for most houses is D with only a small number being either A or B.

4.1.4. Shelf life of a Home Report

The legislation that provides for the Home Report does not prescribe a 'shelf life' specifying a period of time for which it is valid, although it must be no more than 12-weeks old when it goes on the market. If a home has been on the market for more than 12 weeks, a buyer may need to instruct his or her own surveyor to have the house re-surveyed or the valuation refreshed in the later stages of the transaction in order to satisfy his or her lender that it is still a sound basis for lending the money. Alternatively, it may be possible to agree with the seller that he or she has the original survey 'refreshed'. This is likely to be a cheaper option, as far from being an additional survey, it is more likely to involve a simple re-inspection, instructed by the seller, to ensure that the original survey and valuation remain valid. Any instruction to refresh a single survey will be a matter for the buyer and seller to decide and the charge, if any, will be determined by the surveyor or Home Report provider as part of their service. Only the seller can ask the chartered surveyor to refresh or update the report.

4.1.5. What this means for buyers

If you are buying a home, the seller or his or her selling agent (i.e. solicitor or estate agent) must give you a copy of a Home Report within nine calendar days of you asking for it. The seller or selling agent can make a reasonable charge to cover the cost of copying the report and posting it to you. It can also be sent electronically. The seller can only refuse to give potential buyers a copy of the report if:

• he or she believes they are not seriously interested in purchasing the property, or

• he or she believes they don't have sufficient money, or

• they are someone the seller is unlikely to sell the house to, although he or she cannot discriminate against them for reasons that are against the law, that is on the grounds of gender, race, religion or belief, disability, age, sexual orientation or marital/ civil partnership status.

If you are also selling a home, you should read 7.2, which tells you what this means for sellers.

If any repairs are marked as category 2 or category 3, you should consider whether you can cope with the repair works. If there are lots of similar properties on the market, you could just walk away. If you like the property a lot, you should get estimates for completing the works.

There are exceptions to the duty to provide a Home Report. These include:

- houses that have been on the market continuously since before 1 December 2008;

- new housing sold off-plan or to the first occupier;

- newly-converted property not previously used in its converted state;

- right to buy homes;

- dual-use homes used for residential and non-residential purposes;

- seasonal holiday homes as defined in planning legislation (as distinct from second or holiday homes that could be used all year if the owner so chose).

Even if a home does not require a Home Report, the seller will still need to provide potential buyers with a valid energy performance certificate for the house if they request one.

If the seller or his or her solicitor or estate agent won't give you a Home Report, ask your council's trading standards department for help. They can take action against the seller or agent – see 7.2.1.

While the seller commissions the survey, the buyer also has the right to rely on it. If the buyer suffers a material loss because the report does not meet the legal requirements, then he or she has a right to damages. The legal requirements are that the survey report is based on an inspection of the house; has been prepared in a fair and unbiased way; and has been prepared with reasonable skill and care. A material loss has been suffered when the market value of the house on the date of the survey report is materially lower than the value given in the survey report; and the buyer has paid more than the true market value of the house on the date of the survey. For example, if the surveyor missed dry rot in the house, that would lower its value and the buyer, relying on the valuation, may end up paying more than the market value. For information on complaints about surveyors, see 4.3.

4.2. Building survey

This type of survey, which is not required for a Home Report, is a detailed examination of the whole property and its services and is carried out by a chartered building surveyor. It is rarely used in Scotland, partly because of the speed at which home purchase normally takes place and because most sellers are unlikely to allow such a survey unless there is a very limited market for the property and you have expressed a very strong interest. However, if you are thinking of buying a very old or unusual type of property, a property you plan to renovate or alter, or a property that has had extensive alterations, a building survey may be advisable.

The survey is very detailed and could mean some disturbance to the property, such as sawing into timbers to check for rot or drilling into walls to check for dampness. The survey may include or recommend specialist inspection of the drainage, electrical system, central heating and timbers. There may still be some restrictions on access to covered floors and roof spaces but, within these restrictions, the survey will be complete.

Because of the work required for the report, this type of inspection will cost considerably more than a Home Report. The cost may be further increased if tradesmen are brought in to do any work. You should ask the surveyor to tell you the likely price before instructing the survey. If you want the report to include a valuation, you should ask for this when you commission the survey.

4.3. Complaints about chartered surveyors

Sometimes surveyors are negligent: they may miss something about the property that was important which results in loss to the person who relied on the survey. In these circumstances, it may be necessary to take legal action. In other cases, a surveyor's conduct may be unsatisfactory or unprofessional and, in these circumstances, you can complain to the surveyor's firm, his or her professional body or to the Surveyors Ombudsman Service.

Only members of the Royal Institution of Chartered Surveyors (RICS) can call themselves 'a chartered surveyor'. They will have the initials MRICS or FRICS after their names.

If you have a complaint about a firm of chartered surveyors (or one where at least one partner is a chartered surveyor), you should first try to resolve it through the firm's complaints handling procedure. All chartered surveyors' firms must have one and details of how to use it should be included in any correspondence to you. If it is not resolved, you should write to RICS Regulation (see 4.4). Your letter should contain permission for the RICS to send a copy of your complaint and any documents to the firm involved.

The RICS can only investigate complaints alleging professional misconduct, including:

- failure to have or use a complaints handling procedure;

- incompetence;

- allegation or conviction of a criminal offence;

- unjustifiable delay in dealing with your affairs;

- failure to reply to letters;

- disclosure of confidential information;

- failure to disclose a conflict of interest;

- failure to look after your money. Members must keep your money in a separate 'client account' and maintain a record of all transactions.

A conflict of interest may arise if your interests conflict with the private interests of the surveyor or with the interests of another client of the surveyor or their firm. The surveyors must tell you this in writing. You must also be told that this firm cannot act for you until you get separate independent professional advice.

A chartered surveyor who is found to have breached the RICS by-laws or code of conduct can be reprimanded, suspended or expelled from membership. The RICS will not comment on, or investigate, cases where you have a remedy in law, nor will it assess or award compensation. In cases such as alleged professional negligence or breach of contract, or where you believe that you have a claim for compensation, you should consult a citizens' advice bureau (see the phone book) or a solicitor.

Surveyors Ombudsman Service

The Surveyors Ombudsman Service offers a free and independent review of consumer complaints about surveying services provided by chartered surveyors in Scotland who are members of the RICS and estate agents who are members of the service. The ombudsman will only consider a complaint that has not been resolved by the surveyor or estate agent concerned. The ombudsman can investigate:

- possible breaches of a chartered surveyor's or estate agent's legal obligations;

- unfair treatment;

- financial loss;

- maladministration.

These might include:

- avoidable delay;

- failure to follow proper procedures;

- rudeness or discourtesy;

- not explaining matters;

- refusing to deal with a complaint fully or promptly;

- poor service and incompetence.

The ombudsman can award compensation for loss or expenses of up to £25,000 or for stress and inconvenience of up to £500. For further information, see 4.4.

Arbitration

You could also use the Arbitration Procedure for Surveying Disputes or take the firm to court. The arbitration procedure is designed to resolve disputes quickly more cheaply than a court. It is independently administered by IDRS Ltd (see 4.4). While less formal than a court, the decision is legally binding. Before you can use the arbitration procedure, you must first try to resolve your complaint through the firm's in-house complaints handling procedure. All RICS members must agree to arbitration. You will have to pay for this service, which can be quite expensive, so you should first consider the ombudsman service. If your complaint is upheld, the other party must pay the arbiter's fees and any administrator's fees, costs and expenses associated with an arbitration hearing.

4.4 Further information

More information about the Home Report is available on the Scottish Government Home Report website: http://www.homereportscotland.gov.uk

Complaints about chartered surveyors should be addressed to RICS Regulation, Surveyor Court, Westwood Way, Coventry CV4 8JE (tel: 020 7695 1670, e-mail: regulation@rics.org)

Home Report: a guide for buyers and sellers in Scotland is available from the RICS contact centre (tel: 0870 333 1600, e-mail: contactrics@rics.org) or can be downloaded from www.rics.org/homereport

Information on the Surveyors Ombudsman Service is available from the Surveyors Ombudsman Service, PO Box 1021, Warrington, WA4 9FE (tel: 0330 440 1634 or 01925 530270, textphone; 0330 440 1600 or 01925 430886, e-mail: enquiries@surveyors-ombudsman.org.uk, http://www.surveyors-ombudsman.org.uk)

For more information about the Arbitration Procedure for Surveying Disputes, contact IDRS Ltd, 24 Angel Gate, City Road, London EC1V 2PT (tel: 020 7520 3800, e-mail: info@idrs.ltd.uk, http://www.idrs.ltd.uk/business/surveyorsb2b.asp)

Part 5

Buying a home: the legal process

5.1. Making an offer

Once you have decided which property you wish to buy, your solicitor will need to make a formal written offer for it to the seller. The procedure for offering for a newly-built property is described in 5.4.1.

In Scotland, most houses and flats are sold through a system of 'blind bidding'. The seller asks for 'offers over' or 'offers around' the valuation in the single survey report (see 4.1.1). This is an indication of the minimum price the seller expects to fetch. How much you will actually have to pay will depend very much on how busy the market is at that particular time and how much competition there is from other potential buyers. Some properties will be eagerly sought by many buyers because of their size or location. It will usually be possible to find out how much interest there is in a property by asking the seller how many copies of the Home Report have been requested or, more importantly, how many people have noted interest in the property.

Sometimes property is advertised at a fixed price where the seller will accept the first offer for that amount. This may be because there is little activity in the market or the seller is looking for a quick sale. The seller may also offer the property at a fixed price as a starting point for negotiations on price. If you decide to make an offer, your solicitor, based on his or her knowledge of the local market, will be able to guide you on the level at which to pitch your offer. He or she will prepare the offer on your behalf and submit it to the seller's agent (i.e. solicitor or estate agent). If it is accepted without any further negotiation, you will be in a legally-binding contract, so it is essential that your loan arrangements are agreed beforehand.

The closing date

If a number of potential buyers show an interest in a property, the seller's agent will set a time and date – the closing date – for offers to be made. This should allow enough time for interested parties to arrange finance for the purchase. If you are seriously considering making an offer, make sure your solicitor formally notifies the seller's solicitor or estate agent of your interest before you arrange finance (see Part 5), or you may not be informed if a closing date is set.

You will have to decide how much you are prepared to, and can afford to, offer for the property, and how much extra, if any, you are able to add if your offer is in competition with other potential buyers at the closing date. The seller does not have to accept the highest offer but usually will unless it has unacceptable conditions attached. The seller may prefer an offer that has a later or earlier entry date if there is not much between the offers.

If a closing date is not set, that may be because of a lack of interest in the property or simply a slow market and you may be able to negotiate a price for it.

5.2. The missives

Your offer to buy and the seller's acceptance must be made by your respective solicitors. They take the form of an exchange of letters known as missives.

Here are the sorts of things that will be in your offer, which your solicitor should explain to you. It should include a brief description of the property, the proposed date of entry and the price. It should also include any items, such as a cooker or carpets, which you wish to buy from the seller. It will also include a number of conditions, which vary from one transaction to another. The main conditions you should expect include:

• that there are no unusual or unreasonable conditions in the title deeds affecting the property;

- that planning and building control consents and completion certificates required for any alterations will be provided;

- that the street, pavement and main drains are public and maintained by the local authority;

- that there are no proposed road-widening schemes that may affect the property;

- that there are no outstanding statutory notices that affect the property, for example, a notice requiring repair work issued by the council;

- that the seller is genuinely the owner of the property and that his or her right to sell is not restricted in any way.

Your offer should ask the seller to accept it within a specified time. If you are buying a flat, your offer should also include conditions that the maintenance of the common parts is shared fairly, and that there are no outstanding charges for common repairs, for example for work to the roof agreed to by the seller (see outstanding costs in 7.6).

The description

This could simply be the postal address, but if there is a garden, garage, or other outbuildings, then these should be specified in the offer.

The date of entry

This is the date on which you are to be given possession of the property, when you pay the seller the agreed price in exchange for a disposition (the document that transfers the title of the property from the seller to you). If you are relying on the proceeds of the sale of an existing property to help finance the purchase, you should try to get the dates to coincide. If you can't arrange this, you will have to take out a bridging loan to tide you over (see 6.7).

Concluding the missives

The seller may not accept some of your conditions and may wish to vary others, in which case his or her solicitor will send to your solicitor a 'qualified acceptance' of your offer. Your solicitor should explain what the terms of the qualified acceptance mean. Once the conditions and any qualifications are agreed, a formal letter of acceptance is sent and the missives are concluded. You will then have a binding contract.

5.3. Once the missives are concluded

Once you have an agreed contract with the seller, your solicitor will carry out the conveyancing. This is the legal process of transferring the title of the property from the seller to you. It is described at 5.5.

Mortgage and life insurance

If you are taking out a mortgage, you should make sure that an application has been made to the bank or building society and that any linked life insurance is in hand.

Buildings insurance

You should make sure that the property is adequately insured. Depending of the terms of the missives, particularly if you suspect that the seller's insurance may not be adequate, you may need to insure the property from the date of the conclusion of the missives. However, you are not legally required to do so until the date of entry.

Title

You and your spouse, civil partner or partner can buy a home together by offering in both your names and having the title deeds prepared in your joint names. The deeds can provide that on the death of either of you, the title of that person shall pass automatically to the survivor. If you do this, it may affect any will made in the past or future, so you should think carefully about the legal implications of this and discuss them with your solicitor.

Title deeds

The title deeds are the legal documents that set out your rights of ownership of a property, and they may restrict the changes you can make to it. For example, they can prohibit the use of the property for business purposes or specify how the exterior of the building should look.

If you want to do something that is prohibited by a condition in the title deeds, you can apply to the Lands Tribunal for Scotland to change the condition. Your solicitor should be able to do this for you. For more information on the powers of the tribunal and how to make an application, see 5.10.

5.4. Newly-built and newly-converted or renovated properties

The procedure for buying a newly-built home differs from buying an existing one. The home you see advertised may be part of an incomplete estate or may not even have been built yet, and it will usually be offered at a fixed price. Similarly, a conversion or renovation may be offered for sale before the work is complete. With a newly-built home, the builder makes an offer to sell to the buyer.

5.4.1. Newly-built property

Making an offer

Most builders have a standard form of offer that sets out the conditions on which they are prepared to sell. They will not usually vary these as they are designed to impose similar terms on all properties in a development, although some of the conditions may be more in the interests of the developer than those of the buyer. You should make sure that you have arranged your loan and taken legal advice before you accept the builder's offer, because your acceptance is legally binding. You should bear in mind that if the house will take some time to complete, there is a chance that your offer of loan may be withdrawn by your lender. However, you may be able to reserve a home until you are ready to accept the offer by paying the builder a small deposit. It is at the builder's discretion whether to return the deposit if you do not go ahead, so ask before you pay it.

Conditions affecting the use of the property

Normally, you will also be asked to accept, without amendments, a deed of conditions. This sets out what you can and cannot do with your home, with the aim of protecting the appearance and use of the development. Unless they are later changed, you will have the right to require your neighbours to stick to the conditions relating to their properties' appearance and use and they will equally have the right to expect this of you. The title deeds (see 5.3) may also provide for the setting up of a residents' association and may contain arrangements for the maintenance of common areas and say who should carry out the work, such as a landscape maintenance company. Your solicitor will explain the terms in the deeds.

Stage payments

When you offer to buy a home that is not yet built, the builder may ask for stage payments. If you are buying with a mortgage, the lender will usually agree to release stage payments at certain stages. The stages depend on the type of construction and the lender's policy. The lender's surveyor will inspect each stage before payment, and you will have to pay the surveyor's fees. You should make sure that the stage payments in the builder's standard offer and the lender's mortgage offer coincide.

National House-Building Council Buildmark scheme

Buildmark is a ten-year warranty and protection scheme offered by NHBC-registered builders. It is not a guarantee. It protects you against the builder going bankrupt before the home is completed, provides an undertaking to repair faulty work within the first two years and insures against major damage of defined types and defects in the drainage for a further eight years.

Zurich Insurance Building Guarantee

This warranty is offered by builders registered with Zurich Insurance. From your acceptance of the builder's offer, it protects you against loss of money paid as a deposit in the event that the builder is unable to complete the contract due to liquidation, bankruptcy or fraud. It also provides ten years' cover against major structural damage and in year nine you can apply for an extension for a further five years. Acceptance will depend on the claims history. During the first two years of ownership, the builder is responsible for all damage and defects, as defined by the policy.

Premier Guarantee for New Homes

This guarantee is offered by builders registered with MD Insurance Services Limited. It protects you against loss of money paid as a deposit in the event that the builder is unable to complete the contract due to liquidation, bankruptcy or fraud, against defects for which the builder is responsible for two years and against major structural damage for a further eight years.

The NHBC scheme provides for arbitration by the Chartered Institute of Arbitrators of disputes that cannot be settled by conciliation. During the defects period, the Premier Guarantee provides for adjudication of disputes by the Royal Institution of Chartered Surveyors. If the builder does not accept the findings or fails to remedy the defect, the Premier Guarantee will meet the claim. As members of the Association of British Insurers, NHBC, Zurich Insurance and MD Insurance Services are bound by the ABI code of practice on complaints about insurance matters and complaints can also be made to the Financial Ombudsman Service. Details of the procedures for arbitration are available from the NHBC (see 3.14). There is no charge to complain to the ombudsman but arbitration might involve a fee and possible costs if you lose.

5.4.2. Newly-converted and renovated property

A home that has just been converted or renovated will not comply with the same building standards as a newly-built home. For example, the window frames in a new home are factory treated against wet rot, while in a conversion, if the frames are sound, a builder probably won't replace them. Also, a new home may be better soundproofed and insulated than a converted or renovated one. However, all of the work will have to comply with the Building Standards Regulations, which require much higher standards than you would find in an older home.

NHBC-registered builders may offer a conversion and renovations warranty if the work complies with the NHBC standards. This covers most aspects of the building and is aimed at ensuring that a sound job is done, rather than a superficial cosmetic exercise. The warranty obliges the builder to put right any defects reported during the first two years and provides insurance cover for builder bankruptcy either before the work is completed or during the first two years, and against major damage of defined types for the remainder of the ten-year period.

Zurich Insurance-registered builders may offer a warranty policy on conversions. While the cover is similar to that on newly-built homes (see 5.4.1), the builder's responsibility for defects is limited to the first year of ownership. It also protects against the loss of money paid as a deposit if the builder is unable to complete the contract due to liquidation, bankruptcy or fraud.

The Premier Guarantee offered on newly-built property by builders registered with MD Insurance Service Limited (see 5.4.1) may also be offered on newly-converted and renovated property.

5.5. Conveyancing

5.5.1. Introduction

Conveyancing is the process of transferring the title (ownership) of a property from the seller to the buyer. It starts as soon as the missives are concluded and you have a 'bargain', that is, a legally-binding contract. Therefore, conveyancing is involved whether you are buying or selling or both. While it is theoretically possible to do the work yourself, conveyancing is a complex process that involves the most valuable asset you are likely to own. If you are taking out a mortgage, your lender will not, as a general rule, agree to you doing your own conveyancing. It is therefore safer to use a solicitor to do the work.

Traditionally, solicitors have carried out the legal work in buying and selling property. In addition, many offer an estate agency service or belong to a solicitors' property centre or both (see 7.3). You could also use a qualified conveyancer, who is not a solicitor but is qualified to carry out conveyancing. He or she must be registered with the Law Society of Scotland, which is responsible for setting standards for training and qualifications and for carrying out disciplinary functions. Most qualified conveyancers are employed by firms of solicitors. If you want to find an independent qualified conveyancer, you can get the names and addresses from the Law Society of Scotland or Registers of Scotland Executive Agency (see 5.10). Further references to solicitors in this chapter apply equally to qualified conveyancers.

A solicitor cannot act for two parties where his or her interests conflict or where there is a serious possibility that a conflict may arise, such as between a buyer and a seller.

You will be asked to sign documents at various stages of the process. Make sure that you are given an explanation of the meaning of any documents and that you understand them before you sign.

Unless you are a first-time buyer, the conveyancing involved in buying is usually carried out in parallel with the conveyancing involved in selling. If you are moving locally, your solicitor will carry out both procedures. However, if you are moving out of the area, you may find it more useful and convenient to use a local solicitor to do the conveyancing for your purchase.

Once you have a legally-binding contract, your solicitor will investigate the property and its title. This is done by asking the seller's solicitor to provide any relevant information, supported by documents, including items such as planning permission, building warrants and guarantees referred to in the property questionnaire part of the Home Report (see 4.1). Your solicitor will get the deeds, including the title deeds and any deed of conditions that applies to the property, from the seller's solicitor and do the following.

- check the land certificate and the deeds to make sure that the seller actually owns the property, and that the deeds are free from defects and do not contain any unusual or unreasonable conditions that will affect your use of the property;

- tell you about any burdens (limitations or legal restrictions) or servitudes (obligations to allow someone to use the land or prevent you from making use of it) that affect the property;

- check the rights of any third parties to enforce conditions that affect the property;

- ask the local authority and water and sewerage authority whether there are any impending plans that might affect the property;

- make sure that the ground burdens, such as property management fees or maintenance charges for a common garden, are properly divided between you and the seller;

- ensure that any existing standard security (mortgage) over the property is discharged when the property is transferred to you.

5.5.2. Standard security

This is the legal agreement that grants security over the property to your lender, if you have a mortgage. This means that if you don't keep up the loan repayments, the lender would be able to sell your home to recover the amount lent to you. If you are buying the property jointly with someone else, you will both / all be equally liable to pay the mortgage repayments, and if one person defaults on payment, the lender can take action against the other owners to pay that person's share. The agreement has to be drawn up by a solicitor, and can normally be done by your solicitor, as long as your lender agrees to this. Although the work is being done for your lender, you are the one that pays for it, so it will be cheaper for you if your own solicitor can do it. So, check whether your lender will use your solicitor before instructing him or her. When the document is ready, you will have to sign it.

If you are married, or in a civil partnership and are buying the house in your name only, your solicitor must get your spouse's or civil partner's consent to grant the standard security to your lender.

5.5.3. Occupancy rights

When a husband and wife or civil partners live together, but only one of them owns the home, the other has the right to live in it. Similarly, when a man and a woman are (or were) living together as if they were husband and wife, but only one of them owns the home and the other has been granted occupancy rights by a court, they have the right to live in it for the period granted by the court. Your solicitor will check that there are no outstanding rights that could affect the transfer of ownership to you. If the seller is divorced or was in a civil partnership that was dissolved, your solicitor will check that no applications have been made to a court for a transfer of the property under the Family Law (Scotland) Act 1985.

5.5.4. The disposition

This is the legal document that transfers ownership of the property from the seller to you. Your solicitor drafts it and agrees its terms with the seller's solicitor. The seller will sign the document before the settlement so that the disposition, the deeds and the keys can be exchanged for your solicitor's cheque for the full purchase price on the date of entry.

5.5.5. Settlement

This is when you get possession of the property, and usually happens on the agreed date of entry. To do this, your solicitor will certify to your lender that the title is good; get the loan cheque from your lender; and obtain from you your contribution to the purchase price (see 5.8). In exchange for the cheque for the purchase price, your solicitor receives the disposition and other title documents, and the keys. The property is then yours. If you have a lender, it will retain the deeds as security over the property. If you don't have a lender you should ask your solicitor to put them in safekeeping.

5.6. When you get the keys

Normally, the keys will be handed over as part of the settlement package in exchange for your solicitor's cheque for the full purchase price.

When you get the keys, there are a number of checks that you should make as soon as possible. You should check that all the items set out in the missives are there and that services, such as gas, electricity, water, gas fires, electrical appliances and central heating are in working order. If anything is missing or not working, contact your solicitor immediately, or you may lose your contractual rights.

It is the seller's responsibility to take final readings of gas and electricity meters but you should make a note of the readings when you get the keys so that you can check them against your first bills.

It may be difficult to check whether everything is working if the seller has not left operating instructions for the central heating system and other appliances. It's a good idea to go and see the seller in the run-up to the date of entry, and ask him or her to show you how to operate the central heating (and security system if there is one), where the electricity and gas meters are, and the stopcock to the water supply. If there are any appliances, such as a cooker or dishwasher, included in the sale, ask for any user's manuals or instruction booklets, and also for any guarantees or service agreements. However, remember that some agreements are not transferable.

If you are moving into a home that is newly-built or newly-converted by a member of the National House-Building Council, or one that is still covered by an NHBC warranty, make sure that you get a copy of the *Guide to your New Home*.

If you are moving into a home that is newly-built or newly-converted by a Zurich Insurance-registered builder, make sure you are given the insurance certificate, a copy of the policy document and *Get on Board: the Home Owner's Guide*. If a Zurich Insurance warranty is being transferred to you, make sure you notify Zurich Insurance of the change of ownership (see 3.14).

If you are moving into a home that is newly-built or newly-converted by a Premier Guarantee-registered builder, make sure you get the certificate of insurance and summary of the cover.

5.7. After settlement

5.7.1. Registration

After the settlement, your solicitor will register your ownership of the property and the standard security in favour of your lender in the Land Register of Scotland. The Land Register contains details of:

• the property's current ownership;

• the area it covers, on the Ordnance Survey map;

• charges (securities or mortgages);

• title conditions affecting it.

The register's accuracy is guaranteed by the state.

5.7.2. Your title deeds

If you have a mortgage, your lender will probably retain the original copies of your deeds. If you don't have a mortgage, you should ask your solicitor to put them in safekeeping. The Land Register entries are based on the title deeds and if an entry is later questioned, or it is alleged that a mistake has been made, it may be necessary to refer back to the original deeds. Therefore, it is wise to retain them. Although not all deeds and documents need to be kept, you should ask your solicitor for advice as to which are important to keep.

5.8. Costs

There are two elements to the costs: professional conveyancing fees and outlays. When you engage a solicitor, he or she must write to you at the earliest opportunity with an estimate of his or her total fee, including VAT and outlays, or the basis on which the fee will be charged. If you are buying and selling and using the same solicitor to do all the conveyancing, you may be offered a package deal on fees. Similarly, if you are using a solicitor to sell your property and do the conveyancing, you may be offered a package to cover the sale commission and conveyancing fees. If your mortgage lender is prepared to use your solicitor to prepare the standard security, as is normally the case, this will reduce your costs.

Conveyancing fees

A solicitor's fees and commission are not fixed but are open to negotiation, so you should shop around. The main factors he or she will take into account are the time involved in doing the work and the value of the property. The lowest fee is not a guarantee of the best service. If you choose a cheaper service, you may not get the same degree of personal service or the face-to-face advice that you may get elsewhere, so you should decide what is important to you. The fees should cover the following services:

- preliminary work, including making the offer and exchanging missives, leading up to the conclusion of the bargain;

- conveyancing;

- handling the legal work connected with the loan part of the transaction.

As a general rule, a solicitor who has received money from you should put it in some sort of interest bearing account for you. This, however, depends on the amount of money being held: smaller sums (less than £500), which should be paid out within two months, are not required to earn interest; larger sums, even for a short period, are.

Outlays

The costs outwith your solicitor's control are fees and taxes payable to the government, such as the fees due to Registers of Scotland, search fees and, where applicable, stamp duty land tax. The outlays that you will have to pay should be set out in the letter from your solicitor detailing the fees and outlays payable.

If you are taking out a loan, you may have to pay arrangement or mortgage indemnity fees or both (see 6.6 for more information on this).

Registration fees

A fee is charged for an application to register the disposition in the Land Register. The fee is based on the amount of money paid for a property. This ranges from £30 for a transaction of up to £50,000 to £7,500 for a transaction in excess of £5,000,000. The fee for registering the standard security is £30.

The fees are revised periodically. See 5.10 for where to obtain details of current fees.

Stamp duty land tax

This is a government tax on the purchase of a property that has to be paid where the price exceeds £125,000. The rate of duty is 1 per cent for prices of £125,001 to £250,000, 3 per cent for prices of £250,001 to £500,000 and 4 per cent for prices over £500,000. The tax is due on the full value, not just the excess over £125,000. Until 31 December 2009, the 1 per cent rate applies to prices of £175,001 to £250,000, after which the rate will revert to prices over £125,000 unless the government decides to continue the higher rate. If the property is in a disadvantaged area, the 1 per cent duty applies to prices from £150,001 to £250,000. Until 31 December 2009, the disadvantaged area relief is therefore superseded. See 5.10 for further information on these areas. If you are buying under the right to buy scheme (see 3.2), you pay duty on the discounted price, if applicable. You can save on the amount of duty to be paid if the purchase price includes items of furniture or appliances that can be distinguished from the price of the property.

If you buy a newly built zero-carbon home (that is a home that generates the energy needed to run it by using equipment such as combined heat and power boilers, fuel cells, solar panels or wind turbines) costing up to £500,000, it is exempt from stamp duty land tax.

When will payment be due?

You will normally be asked to pay for outlays, as and when they become due during the transaction, although most fees are usually paid at settlement. Where you are selling, your solicitor will normally deduct the fees and outlays from the proceeds of sale. Your solicitor is entitled to expect payment of his or her fees at settlement but you may be able to come to a different arrangement.

5.9. Complaints

Sometimes solicitors are negligent – they may do something that results in loss to the person who relied on their services. In other cases, their services may be unsatisfactory, inadequate or unprofessional. What you do depends on the type of complaint.

Professional services

You should let your solicitor know right away if you are unhappy with any aspect of his or her professional services. If you are unable to resolve the matter, take it up with the firm's client relations partner. Every solicitor's firm must have a written procedure for dealing with complaints. If you are still unable to resolve the matter, contact the Scottish Legal Complaints Commission (see 5.10). The commission will decide whether the complaint is about the service provided or the solicitor's conduct. It will deal with complaints about service and refer complaints or any aspect of a complaint about conduct to the Law Society of Scotland (see 5.10).

The Law Society of Scotland has powers to deal with complaints about professional misconduct and excessive fees and in appropriate cases can award compensation. In more serious cases of professional misconduct, not involving a claim of negligence, it will prosecute the solicitor before the Scottish Solicitors Discipline Tribunal.

Negligence

Negligence may occur when a solicitor does not exercise a reasonable standard of skill and care and the client suffers a loss because of this, for example, by failing to register documents. All solicitors are required to have insurance to cover any compensation awarded for negligence. If you consider that your solicitor has been negligent then you will need independent legal advice from a citizens' advice bureau or another solicitor if you wish to pursue such a claim. The Law Society of Scotland does not handle negligence claims.

The Law Society of Scotland maintains a list of solicitors who are prepared to advise on negligence claims against other solicitors (see 5.10).

5.10 Further information

For information on the Lands Tribunal for Scotland, contact The Clerk to the Lands Tribunal for Scotland, George House, 126 George Street, Edinburgh EH2 4HH (tel: 0131 271 3450, e-mail: mailbox@lands-tribunal-scotland.org.uk, http://www.lands-tribunal-scotland.org.uk/).

Accessing our services, which gives details of literature, products and services, is available from Registers of Scotland Executive Agency:

The Edinburgh Customer Services Unit, Erskine House, 68 Queen Street, Edinburgh EH2 4NF (tel: 0845 607 0161) or Glasgow Customer Services Centre, 9 George Square, Glasgow G2 1DY (tel: 0845 607 0164) or http://www.ros.gov.uk/pdfs/info.pdf. For both offices e-mail: customer.services@ros.gov.uk.

You can also get details of qualified conveyancers from the customer services centres or at http://www.ros.gov.uk/aboutus/conveyancers.html.

For information about the services provided by solicitors, details of local solicitors who do conveyancing work or independent qualified conveyancers, or about complaints procedures, contact the Law Society of Scotland, 26 Drumsheugh Gardens, Edinburgh EH3 7YR (tel: 0131 226 7411, regulation liaison department helpline: 0845 113 0018, e-mail: reg@lawscot.org. uk, http://www.lawscot.org.uk).

Details of postcodes qualifying for the stamp duty relief in disadvantaged areas can be found at http://www.hmrc.gov. uk/so/dar/scotland.pdf or from the HM Revenue & Customs stamp taxes helpline on tel: 0845 603 0135.

The Scottish Legal Complaints Commission can be contacted at The Stamp Office, 10–14 Waterloo Place, Edinburgh EH1 3EG (tel: 0131 528 5111, e-mail: enquiries@scottishlegalcomplaints. org.uk, http://www.scottishlegalcomplaints.org.uk/).

Part 6
Mortgages

6.1. Introduction

Most people buying a home need to take out a loan – a mortgage – to help pay for it. How much you need to borrow will depend on your personal circumstances, such as your financial circumstances and your age. A mortgage is likely to be your biggest and most important financial commitment, and it will be secured on your home. This means that the lender could sell your home if you don't keep up the loan repayments. So you need to be sure that you can afford the commitment or you will risk losing it. You should also allow for the other costs involved in buying a home – legal expenses, stamp duty land tax, registration fees and removal expenses – and consider taking out mortgage payment protection insurance (see 6.9) in case you get into difficulties with your mortgage payments.

Mortgages are available from a variety of lenders, such as building societies, banks, insurance companies, finance houses and specialist mortgage companies. If you are buying under your right to buy (see 3.2) and you have difficulty in arranging a mortgage, you can apply to your landlord for a loan.

When considering how much you can afford to borrow, and what type of loan would suit your circumstances, you may wish to get independent financial advice.

The sale and administration of mortgages is regulated by the Financial Services Authority (FSA) and the Mortgage Conduct of Business Rules which lenders and brokers are subject to.

An independent financial adviser can advise on a range of financial products, such as insurance or investments, as opposed to a tied adviser who can only advise on one company's products. You should always shop around for advice. An independent financial adviser who advises on mortgages must have a specialist mortgage qualification and be authorised by the FSA to advise on mortgages. There are also specialist mortgage brokers who simply advise on mortgages. Financial advisers are regulated by the FSA. You should check that any financial adviser you propose using is registered with the FSA and is independent. For more information, see 6.10.

These are some of the key questions you should ask of any prospective lender:

- Does the cost of the loan vary depending on whether you take out any linked purchases, such as buildings or life insurance?

- What are the costs and implications of transferring your mortgage from one lender to another? You should ask this of both any existing and any prospective lender.

- Can you use an existing life insurance policy as security for an interest-only mortgage? (see 6.3.2).

- What fees and costs are involved and what is the total amount payable?

All of these questions and others should be covered by the 'key features' document that the lender is required to produce when you enquire about a particular mortgage product.

6.2. How much can you borrow?

You should plan your finances at an early stage so that you do not over-commit yourself. Ask a potential lender how much it would allow you to borrow, but be warned that what a lender may lend you and what you can afford to borrow may not be the same. There are two factors it will consider: your income and the percentage of the valuation of the property in the Home Report that it would lend.

The amount you can borrow will usually be up to three-and-a-half times your gross annual earnings but may also take into account your other financial commitments. If you want a joint loan, most lenders will normally include the lower earner's salary.

The amount you can afford to borrow should take into account your current disposable income and how that may be affected in the future. For example, if you take out a joint loan based on your earnings and those of your partner or spouse, how will that be affected if you start a family and one of you takes time out of employment? When calculating how much they are prepared to lend you, lenders must carry out an affordability assessment on you.

So, before you start to look for a home, you should find out, in principle, how much you could borrow. Don't forget that the property's valuation may be less than the price you propose to pay and, if so, you will have to find the difference. For example, if you want to pay £250,000 for a property, which is valued at £240,000 and you are offered an 80 per cent mortgage, that will be a mortgage of £192,000 (240,000 x 80% = 192,000). You will have to find the difference of £58,000, and all the other costs of the purchase.

If the property needs essential repairs to bring it up to the standard the lender requires, part of the mortgage may be withheld until you have carried these out.

6.3. Types of mortgages

A mortgage has two elements: the capital, which is the amount of money you borrow; and the interest, which is the money charged on the capital until you pay it back. There are different ways you can repay a mortgage: repayment or interest–only or a combination of the two. You will need to decide which is best for you.

- *Repayment mortgage.* You make regular payments, usually monthly, of capital and interest.

- *Interest-only mortgage.* You make regular payments of the interest on the loan, which do not reduce the amount of the loan. You must arrange some other way to repay the loan at the end of its term, for example through an investment or savings plan.

You can always repay the loan before the end of the period for which it was arranged, although there may be an additional charge, depending upon the type of mortgage product selected, especially if you do so within a few years of arranging it. You can pay off lump sums from time to time, or make regular overpayments if you have a 'flexible' mortgage (see 6.4.2), so reducing the period of payment. The shorter that period, the less your total interest bill.

6.3.1. Repayment mortgage

This is the simplest type of mortgage. You have one contract, with the lender, to whom you make regular repayments of capital and interest during the term of the loan. In the early years, these will be mainly interest but as the outstanding capital decreases, more of your payments go towards repaying the capital as the interest decreases.

The loan is usually paid off over 20 to 25 years. However, if you do not have as long as this before retiring, a lender may only offer you a shorter loan period. In certain circumstances some lenders may be prepared to extend the term beyond 20 to 25 years, particularly for first-time buyers, to make the purchase more affordable.

6.3.2. Interest-only mortgage

With this type of mortgage, there are two elements. The first is a contract with the lender, to whom you repay only the interest over the period of the loan. The second is a savings plan, such as an individual savings account, or an investment, such as a pension plan, that repays the capital at the end of the loan.

- *Individual savings account mortgage.* You pay only the interest during the period of the loan. At the same time, you make regular payments into an individual savings account (ISA), and at the end of the mortgage period, you cash it in to pay off the full loan. There is currently a limit of £7,200 on the amount you can invest in an ISA in each tax year. The value of ISAs depends on their value on the stock market, which can go down as well as up. Therefore, you run a risk that at the end of the mortgage period, your investment may not be worth enough to pay off the loan and you will have to find the difference. Because the ISA value is building up during the loan, a lender will probably require you to take out a life insurance policy for the amount of the mortgage in case you die before the end of the projected period of the loan. That makes this type of mortgage more expensive overall. A benefit of an ISA mortgage is that currently the proceeds of your investment are tax free.

• *Personal pension plan mortgage.* If you are self-employed or have a personal pension plan, you can link a mortgage to the pension plan. As with ISA mortgages, you pay only the interest during the period of the loan. At the same time, you make payments to a pension plan, which at the end of the loan period is designed to pay off the full loan and provide you with a pension. You can only use the lump sum element of your pension plan to pay off the loan, and there is no guarantee that its value will be enough. If there is a shortfall, you will have to find the difference. This type of mortgage can offer substantial tax advantages. You can claim tax relief on your payments to the pension plan, and the lump sum you get when you retire is tax free.

If you are considering one of these mortgages, you should get independent financial advice (see 6.1), and you should check that the plan or investment grows enough so that at the end of the term you have enough to pay off the loan.

6.4. Mortgage features

Mortgages can have different features, for example:

6.4.1. Cash back

You will get a cash payment, usually between 3 per cent and 5 per cent, from the lender. The higher the cash payment, the greater and more complex the number of strings that are likely to be attached. You may be faced with high redemption penalties over several years and you may also be offered a less competitive interest rate than is available elsewhere.

6.4.2. Flexible

This gives you some scope to change your monthly payments to suit your ability to pay. It is also useful if you want to pay off your loan more quickly. Several flexible features are becoming common, including:

- Overpayments – you can pay more than your normal monthly mortgage payment or pay off a lump sum, or both.

- Underpayments and payment holidays – you pay less than the normal monthly payment for a limited period (say six or twelve months). You may even be able to stop making payments altogether. This could be useful if, say, you lose your job or take time off to care for a child.

- Borrow extra (loan drawdown) – you can borrow extra without further approval from your lender, provided the total loan does not go above an overall limit. Alternatively you may be able to 'borrow back' against earlier overpayments.

6.4.3. Offset

With an offset mortgage, your main current account or savings account (or both) are linked to your mortgage. Each month, the amount you owe on your mortgage is reduced by the amount in these accounts before working out the interest due on the loan. So, as your current account and savings balances go up, you pay less on your mortgage, and as they go down, you pay more.

6.4.4. Current account

A current account mortgage is similar to an offset mortgage in that it offsets the balance of your savings against your mortgage. However, rather than your mortgage and current account being separate pots of money, they are usually combined into one account. This means that the account acts like one big overdraft.

6.5. Interest rates

Whatever type of loan you choose, the interest rate is very important. All lenders will quote an annual percentage rate (APR), which is an approved system to help you compare the cost of the credit. The APR takes into account the added costs of a loan, such as arrangement fees and solicitor's charges. Generally, the higher the APR, the more expensive the credit. Some APRs will reflect short-term discounted or fixed rates, so you should check the monthly repayments and the sum paid over the whole term of the loan, and not just the initial APR.

While the general interest rates charged by lenders will be similar, many offer incentives for first-time buyers or to persuade you to switch to them, so you should shop around. Your solicitor or other independent adviser can help you. Some terms you may come across are as follows:

- *Variable rate.* Interest rates on deposits and mortgages vary according to the base rate (the rate, determined by banks, on which they base their lending rates of interest). Some lenders adjust the interest rate each time the base rate varies, others review your repayments annually, or you may be able to choose. This is usually the lender's standard rate and it is generally worth looking at other options, as they may be cheaper.

- *Fixed rate.* The interest rate is set for a fixed period, for example, two, five or ten years and possibly even longer. This may help you to budget but it could be an expensive option if the general interest rate falls below the fixed rate. Unless the rate is fixed until the end of the mortgage, you are usually charged the lender's standard variable rate at the end of the fixed rate.

- *Capped-rate and collared-rate.* On a capped rate, the interest rate will not rise above an agreed maximum for a given period but will fall in line with the base rate. On a collared rate, the interest will not fall below an agreed minimum for a given period but will rise in line with the base rate. These may be combined in a cap and collar-rate loan. At the end of the period, you are usually charged the lender's standard variable rate.

• *Discounted interest-rate.* Many lenders offer new borrowers a discount of 1 per cent or more on the standard variable rate for a year or more.

• *Tracker rate.* The interest rate is a set amount above or below the Bank of England or some other base rate. It always tracks changes in that rate.

If you have a repayment mortgage on a variable interest rate and the interest rate increases, you may be able to extend the period of the loan, rather than increase your repayments.

6.6. Fees and penalties

All mortgage-related fees will be set out in the 'key features' documents. They may include any of the fees described in this section.

Most lenders charge an arrangement fee for setting up capped, discounted, tracker or fixed-rate mortgages (see section 5 in the key features document). This could be as much as £600, or more in some cases.

If you decide to change from a fixed, capped-rate, collared-rate, tracker or cash-back mortgage during the agreed period your lender is likely to make an early redemption charge, which can be from one to six months' interest (see section 10 in the 'key features' documents). In addition, the lender may make a redemption charge if you change within a certain period after the agreed period. You may be better off staying in the scheme for the agreed period and then think about changing.

With a cash-back mortgage, the lender may require you to take out the insurance that it offers, and the cash-back payment may affect your liability for Capital Gains Tax.

Some lenders may require a mortgage indemnity guarantee. They may also refer to it as a high percentage loan fee, high lending fee or additional security fee. This is a one-off premium, which is paid along with your first mortgage payment, that you pay to protect your lender (not you) if you fall significantly behind on your mortgage payments and it has to repossess your property and sell it. You may have to pay this if the value of your mortgage is above a threshold of 75 per cent to 80 per cent of the value of the property; this varies depending on the lender. For further information, see 6.11. The premium can be substantial – up to 8 per cent of the amount of the loan over the threshold – so you should check this when working out how much you can afford to borrow.

6.7. Bridging loans

If you are selling your present home and buying a new one, you may find that you have to produce the money to pay for your new home before you have received the proceeds from the sale of your old home. Banks and financial institutions will provide a 'bridging loan' to tide you over this gap.

You will not be able to take on a bridging loan before you have concluded the missives (see 7.5) on the sale of your present home. If you purchase your new home with a bridging loan, you will have to continue paying the mortgage on your present home as well as the interest on the bridging loan for your new home. Bridging loans can be very expensive, and should only be relied on as a temporary measure if at all possible.

6.8. Life insurance

If you have a repayment loan, you should consider taking out a life insurance policy, which can be decreasing term insurance or level term insurance. The cover provided by a decreasing term policy decreases as the capital is repaid. The cover provided by a level term policy is equivalent to the amount of the original advance, irrespective of the actual loan debt. If you have an ISA or personal pension plan loan, the lender will probably require you to take out a level term life insurance policy.

However, while life insurance is of benefit to your lender and your dependents in assuring that your loan is repaid if you die, if you have no dependents, you should consider whether it is of any benefit to you. Also, if you take out a life policy in connection with a pension mortgage, this is likely to increase the amount of the loan fee.

For an initial sum insured of £200,000, a 30-year old non-smoker could expect to pay about £9 per month for a 25-year decreasing term policy or £12 per month for a 25-year level term policy.

6.9. Mortgage payment protection insurance

Your home is at risk if you do not keep up your mortgage payments. A mortgage payment protection policy will help you to pay your monthly mortgage and mortgage-related expenses if you become unemployed, disabled or unable to work but you should check the limitations and exclusions carefully before taking out a policy. There is usually a waiting period, typically 60 to120 days, before you can claim, after which the policy will normally cover your payments for up to 12 or 24 months. Policies will normally cover you against disability until you reach 65 and against unemployment until you reach retirement age or 65, whichever is earlier.

Mortgage payment protection insurance can be a valuable protection for your savings, particularly if you don't qualify for the Support for Mortgage Interest Scheme (see 6.10) or the Homeowners' Mortgage Support Scheme (see 6.10).

You should compare the different policies on offer, as the premiums and cover vary, depending particularly on your occupation and any pre-existing medical conditions. To claim on the unemployment part of the policy typically you must have been employed continuously by the same company for the past 12 months on a permanent contract, so you may not be eligible or cover may be limited if you are self-employed, a sole trader or a contract worker, or it may not cover both parties to a joint loan. You may not be able to claim for an illness you have or have had before, even if it hasn't troubled you for a while. If you are in one of those categories and are offered a policy, you should consider whether the limitations of the cover would provide you with any practical benefit. A mortgage payment protection policy will cost you between £1.60 and £3.00 a month per £100 of monthly payments you want to insure. You may be able to keep the costs down by opting for only one type of cover, for example, unemployment-only cover if your employer provides a high level of sick pay or if you have adequate permanent health insurance. It is strongly recommended that you read the terms of the insurance policy to be clear what is covered, what is excluded, and the amount of any excess.

Some insurance companies offer policies regardless of your lender, and some lenders have special offers of free cover for new borrowers, usually for a limited time. You should shop around to find the best policy for your needs. Many lenders are linked, or 'tied', to particular insurance companies. If you do not wish your choice to be limited in this way, you should get independent financial advice.

6.10. If you get into difficulties

Support for Mortgage Interest Scheme

If you and/or your spouse, civil partner or partner have savings of less than £16,000, or you work less than 16 hours a week or have a spouse, civil partner or partner who works less than 24 hours a week, you can get help from the Support for Mortgage Interest Scheme (SMI) if you become unemployed or cannot work because of a disability. With savings of between £6,000 and £16,000 your support will be affected. If you qualify for SMI, you cannot get any support to help with loan repayments for the first 13 weeks of unemployment or disability. SMI will only help with interest payments. It will not help with repayments of capital or with the premiums of any pension policy that is associated with the loan. The maximum qualifying loan is £200,000.

Homeowners' Mortgage Support Scheme

If you suffer a temporary fall in income, but you expect your financial situation to improve at a later date, this scheme can help you to remain in your home if you are not eligible for Support for Mortgage Interest (see above). Lenders' participation in the scheme is voluntary and the final decision on eligibility for and acceptance into the scheme remains entirely that of the lender. It is open for two years from December 2008, subject to review. For further information, contact a citizens' advice bureau or other advice agency (see the phone book).

The Home Owners' Support Fund

If you are an owner occupier and are in danger of having your home repossessed, the Scottish Government's Home Owners' Support Fund has two schemes that could help you stay in your home.

- The Mortgage to Rent Scheme may be able to help you if you are an owner occupier in financial difficulty and are at least three months in arrears with payments on any loan secured against your home. A social landlord, such as a housing association or local authority, will buy your home and you can continue to live there as a tenant. Funding is available to the landlord so that any necessary repairs can be made to the property and you can be charged a social rent, which is a rent based upon relative property values and local earnings levels. You must get advice from an approved money adviser before you can apply to the scheme, and be able to show that you have explored all options available to you, including discussing your circumstances with your secured lender.

- The Mortgage to Shared Equity Scheme may be able to help you to retain ownership of your home if you are an owner occupier in financial difficulty by reducing your level of debt to a manageable level. To be eligible, you must have at least 25% equity in your home, and be at least three months in arrears with payments on any loan secured against it. You must also have taken appropriate money advice and be able to show that you have explored all options available to you, including discussing your circumstances with your lender, before applying to the scheme. If your circumstances improve in the future, you can buy back the Scottish Government's stake in your home (in part or as a whole), and when it is sold, the Scottish Government will receive its share of the sale price.

For further information, see 6.11.

6.11. Further information

The Financial Services Authority, 25 The North Colonnade, Canary Wharf, London E14 5HS (consumer helpline: 0845 606 1234, minicom/textphone: 08457 300 104). The FSA does not deal with specific consumer complaints, recommend firms or give legal advice. However, the consumer helpline can answer general queries about financial products and services. It can also tell you if a firm is authorised and help 'sign post' you if you have a complaint and don't know whom to contact. The following publications are available from the consumer helpline and the Moneymadeclear website http://www.moneymadeclear.fsa.gov.uk/:

Mortgages
Paying for your mortgage – you can afford a mortgage now, but what if?
Dealing with your mortgage shortfall
Stay in control of your mortgage
House purchase plans

These publications can be downloaded from: http://www.moneymadeclear.fsa.gov.uk/tools/publications/publications.html You can also request hard copies online from:http://www.moneymadeclear.fsa.gov.uk/pubform.aspx

The Council of Mortgage Lenders has consumer information pages on its website http://www.cml.org.uk/cml/consumers (note that some of it is only for home buyers in England and Wales), and further information on mortgage indemnity at http://www.cml.org.uk/cml/consumers/guides/indemnity

The British Association of Insurers has guidance *What does Payment Protection Insurance do?*, which is only available from its website at http://www.abi.org.uk/paymentprotectioninsurance

The Home Owners' Support Fund: Contact the Scottish Government, 4th Floor, Highlander House, 58 Waterloo Street, Glasgow G2 7DA (tel: 0845 279 9999, e-mail: mortgagetorent@scotland.gsi.gov.uk).

Further information on the Home Owners' Support Fund can be found at: http://www.scotland.gov.uk/Topics/Built-Environment/Housing/access/grants/4418

Part 7
Selling your home

7.1. Introduction

If you are selling your home and buying another in Scotland,
you should also read Part 4 on the Home Report and Part 5 on
the legal process of buying a home. This part concentrates on
the procedures not covered in those parts.

7.2. Home Report

You must possess a Home Report before you put your home
on the market. So, before you do so, you should contact
your solicitor or estate agent to arrange for a Home Report
to be prepared. You should shop around for the best Home
Report deal, or ask you solicitor or estate agent to do so, taking
into account factors such as the price, payment arrangements
and which lenders' surveyors panels the surveyor is represented
on. If you plan to do your own advertising and marketing,
see 7.3.

When you put your home on the market, you or your agent
must provide, upon request, a copy of your Home Report (see
Part 4) to a prospective buyer within nine calendar days. You
may make a reasonable charge to cover the costs of copying and
postage. To ensure that your Home Report includes current
information, it must be no more than 12 weeks old when you
put your home on the market. However, in practice, you should
have it prepared immediately before putting it on the market
to ensure that the information is as current as possible at that
point. It would be sensible to include in your Home Report the
surveyor's generic mortgage valuation report (see 4.1.1). Once

it has been prepared, it has no 'shelf life'. You may take the property off the market for up to four weeks on any number of occasions and put it back on the market without having to obtain a new Home Report. In a slow market, however, you may wish to consider having the report 'refreshed' as buyers may be less willing to rely on a report that is more than 12-weeks old.

You can refuse to provide a copy of your Home Report if you reasonably believe that the potential buyer:

• is unlikely to have sufficient money to buy your home;

• is not genuinely interested in buying your home;

• is not a person to whom you are likely to be prepared to sell your home, but this does not allow you to discriminate against him or her for reasons that are against the law, that is on the grounds of gender, race, religion or belief, disability, age, sexual orientation or marital/civil partnership status.

If there is anyone to whom you would not wish to sell your home, you should discuss this with your solicitor or estate agent before putting it on the market. You should ask the selling agent what the cost of the Home Report will be and whether there are any payment options available. You should shop around to find the best available product for your needs.

7.2.1. Penalties for breach of the duty to provide a Home Report

Local authority trading standards services are responsible for enforcement of the duty to provide Home Reports. If an enforcement officer believes that there has been a breach, by a seller or selling agent, of the duties to possess or provide a Home Report, he or she may issue a penalty charge notice. The notice requires payment of a penalty charge, set at £500, within a specified period of time.

A seller or selling agent can appeal against the penalty charge notice and should seek advice from trading standards about how to go about this.

7.2.2. While the report is being prepared

As soon as you decide to sell your home and commission a Home Report, you should ensure that your solicitor inspects your title deeds and has these available for the buyer's solicitor to view. Your solicitor may have to retrieve your title deeds from your lender. You, or someone nominated by you, must complete a property questionnaire, which asks for further information about the house such as alterations, extensions or major works, such as rot treatment, that have been carried out, property management costs and council tax banding. If you don't know the answer to some of the questions you should state this as you must sign the questionnaire stating that it is correct to the best of your knowledge and belief. Make sure that all the necessary documents, such as guarantees and warranties, are available. If any documents are not available, you should discuss this with your solicitor. You should also check with your lender how much money is needed to pay off the loan on the property.

There are a number of other things you should do before putting your home on the market.

• You should discuss your plans with a solicitor (see 5.5.1). Even if you plan to do your own advertising and marketing, it is not usually practicable to do the legal work (see 7.6) yourself without employing a solicitor, as your lender is unlikely to accept it. Your solicitor will get the title deeds from your lender (if you have a loan) and check that you have a good title to the property (see 5.5.1). He or she will also initiate local authority searches to make sure that there are no outstanding notices, orders or proposals affecting the property.

• If you own your home jointly with one or more others, you must get their consent before you can sell. If you are married, and your spouse is not a co-owner, the Matrimonial Homes (Family Protection) (Scotland) Act 1981 requires that you get his or her consent for the sale. Similarly, if you are in a civil partnership, and your partner is not a co-owner, the Civil Partnership Act 2004 requires that you get his or her consent for the sale. Without this consent, you cannot give a purchaser possession of the property. This is particularly important if you are separated from your spouse or civil partner.

Here are some things you might wish to consider before you put your home on the market.

- Is it worth doing any repairs, maintenance or redecorating? Beyond carrying out necessary repairs, don't redecorate unless the home badly needs it. Anyone buying your home may wish to redecorate it to his or her own taste. If you do redecorate, keep to pale, neutral colours.

- Make sure that everything is in working order and that the home is thoroughly cleaned. In particular, if you have central heating, it is worth having your boiler serviced if you do not already have a service plan. If you have a garden, make sure that it is tidy and the grass is cut before people come to view.

- If you have made any changes that required planning permission or building control consent, check that you have the necessary documents and that your solicitor is aware of these, as you will be asked about them in the property questionnaire part of the Home Report. If you have made changes that required permission but you failed to get it at the time, it may be possible to get retrospective permission. Otherwise, you will have difficulty in selling your home. You can check whether you need permission and how to get this by contacting the planning or building control department at your local council.

- You should tell your solicitor about any loans you have taken out that affect the house, aside from your mortgage. These would include, for example, a loan taken out to pay for double glazing, where the documents you have signed mean that the loan is 'secured' against the property.

- If you have had any remedial treatment carried out, for example, for wet or dry rot, or installed a damp-proof course that is covered by a guarantee or insurance, check that the certificates or policies are available and valid, and that the company providing them is still in business, as you will need them for the Home Report. You will also need a description of the work done, such as the original estimate.

7.3. Advertising and marketing your home

You can advertise and market your home yourself or use a selling agent, who could be an estate agent or solicitor. Most solicitors who do residential conveyancing also provide a full estate agency service.

7.3.1. Doing it yourself

If you do not use a selling agent and instead market your own house, you will need to compile a Home Report by instructing a chartered surveyor registered with the Royal Institution of Chartered Surveyors to prepare a single survey with an energy report and you must complete a property questionnaire. Once you have all the documents that you need, you can then market your home. You must provide a copy of your Home Report, upon request, to prospective buyers within nine calendar days, with the exceptions in 7.2. You should also keep a list of everyone you give a Home Report to, as your surveyor will need this information.

Doing your own advertising and marketing will save you the cost of a selling agent's commission but you will have to spend some money on advertising and put your own time into it, and you will not have access to the same range of advertising options.

How much should you ask for? The single survey report in your Home Report will include a market valuation (see 4.1.1). Depending on how busy the local market is and how much competition you think there may be for your property, you can ask for 'offers over' or 'offers around' the valuation price – see 5.1.

Some newsagents and supermarkets have notice boards where you can put up a card. Your employer may have one. You can advertise in the local or national (Scottish) press and on property websites. Use the descriptions given in the property pages as a guide to describing your own home.

You could prepare a typewritten property description sheet to hand out to viewers. For guidance, visit some estate agents and collect property description sheets for properties similar to yours.

Avoid flowery language and describe the property accurately and truthfully. Decide what you want to include in the asking price. For example, carpets, curtains, appliances and furniture that you don't want to take with you could be included, or listed separately at a fixed price or at a price to be negotiated.

To go with your Home Report, you should provide the name, address and phone number of your solicitor to whom expressions of interest and formal written offers should be made. Send a copy of your Home Report to your solicitor.

A 'For Sale' sign is useful for alerting people who may be looking around your area for properties for sale and it will help people who have already contacted you to find you. To avoid being pestered by people calling without an appointment, put your phone number on the sign and 'By appointment only'.

7.3.2. Using an agent

There are advantages in using an agent, which could be an estate agent or a solicitor:

- they can arrange the preparation of your Home Report and send it to potential buyers, although you will be responsible for completing the property questionnaire;

- they have experience of the local market and the potential value of your home;

- solicitors have access to their local solicitors' property centres and other selling routes and can also do the conveyancing;

- some estate agents have links with legal firms that can do the conveyancing;

- they can advertise and market your home more extensively than you can;

- as well as having a shop front, they are likely to have a bank of potential buyers prior to marketing;

- they will deal with enquiries from buyers and arrange viewing appointments

- they should follow up potential buyers and keep you informed of progress;

- they should have contacts to arrange a mortgage for a potential buyer, if necessary;

- if necessary, you can ask for an agent's representative to accompany viewers.

By law, estate agents must:

- give you their terms in writing and say whether they are acting as a multi, joint or sole agent;

- explain their fees;

- declare any personal or connected interests;

- report any offers (unless the seller instructs otherwise) in writing quickly;

- have separate accounts for clients' money;

- not misrepresent any offers.

Solicitors, when carrying out estate agency work, are subject to the same regulatory rules and codes of conduct and service of the Law Society of Scotland (see 5.9) as when doing legal work. They include, for example:

- communicating clearly and effectively with you in clear and simple language;

- giving you in writing details of the work to be carried out and their costs, including fees;

- explaining their fees;

- telling you of any significant developments, such as the cost of the work being more than was estimated;

- telling you about any personal or connected interests;

- telling you about any payments they receive for referring you to others, such as a mortgage broker;

- reporting any offers (unless the seller instructs otherwise) in writing quickly;

- having a separate account for your money.

An agent will prepare the property description for your home, advertise and market it for sale, deal with enquiries and advise you on offers.

If you use an estate agent, you can give sole agency rights to one agent or instruct as many as you wish. The commission is usually about 1.5 per cent of the selling price, although with sole agency rights, you may be able to negotiate a lower commission. You should shop around. Ask for a written estimate of the total charges, including commission, advertising and VAT. The agent will pass any formal offers to your solicitor.

If you use an estate agent, it is a good idea to find one who is a member of the National Association of Estate Agents. All estate agents must also belong to an estate agents' redress scheme (see 7.7). This means that if you complain and the agent does not deal with your complaint to your satisfaction, you can contact the relevant redress scheme and it will investigate the matter further. See 7.8 for how to get a list of member agents in your area.

A solicitor will either advertise and market your property himself or herself or register it with a local solicitors' property centre. The centre will charge a fee to cover display of the property details and an insert in its property listing, mailing list or website. The solicitor will charge a commission of about 1.5 per cent of the selling price in addition to the conveyancing fees. Some solicitors may charge a lower commission or offer a package to cover selling and conveyancing for your sale and also your purchase, so you should shop around and ask for estimates. Once you have engaged a solicitor, he or she must write to you at the earliest opportunity with an estimate of the total fee, including VAT and outlays, or the basis on which the fee will be charged.

7.4. Fixing a closing date

The closing date is the time and date on which formal written offers must be submitted to your solicitor. If you use an estate agent, the offers will usually be sent to them.

Whether you fix a closing date depends on the amount of activity in the housing market and the level of interest in your property. If there is little interest, or the market is very quiet, you will have to decide how long to wait for expressions of interest to accumulate or whether to let it be known that you will consider an individual offer. If you wait too long, potential buyers may find another property. You should get guidance from your agent on this.

You should only fix a closing date when several people have made formal expressions of interest to your solicitor. You should resist offers for a quick sale if there are several people interested in buying.

7.5. Accepting an offer and concluding the missives

You do not have to accept the highest offer made at the closing date, or indeed any offer at all. Usually, the offer will include a number of conditions to suit the person making the offer. These would include the date of entry, and any items to be included in the price, such as carpets and curtains, and technical conditions about, for example, the information in your property questionnaire and any associated planning permission, building control consent, guarantees and warranties.

It is up to you to decide which offer you want to accept. While usually you will want to accept the highest offer, other conditions, such as the date of entry, may also be important you. If the highest offer comes with conditions you don't want to accept, then your solicitor will find out whether there is any room for negotiation. If you are not happy with the conditions, you will then have to decide whether to accept the next highest offer. You could also decide not to accept any of the offers, and re-advertise.

Your agent, if you have one, will normally deal with the main conditions in the offer including the price, the date of entry and the extras that will be included in the sale (such as carpets and curtains). They may negotiate on your behalf to try and change the date of entry and inclusions. If the property is sold at a closing date they will not be able to negotiate on the sale price.

Once you have made a decision, the offer will be passed on to your solicitor (if he or she is not also your selling agent) who will discuss the offer terms with you in more detail before issuing a letter known as a qualified acceptance, which sets out your acceptance of the offer, subject to those conditions that need to be changed (see also 5.2).

Usually, there will then be an exchange of letters (missives) in which your solicitor will try to vary any unacceptable conditions. Normally, this only takes a few days, but sometimes takes longer if there are any unusual conditions in either the offer or qualified acceptance. Once both sides agree, the missives are concluded, and at that stage there is a binding agreement between you. Until the missives are concluded, either party can withdraw without penalty.

7.6. Once the missives are concluded

Once the missives are concluded, your solicitor will do the conveyancing, which is the legal transfer of the title from you to the buyer. The procedures for doing the conveyancing for a sale are similar to those for a purchase (see 5.5) but from the other side of the transaction. They mainly involve your solicitor responding to the buyer's solicitor's enquiries. Your solicitor will also agree the disposition drafted by the buyer's solicitor and arrange for the repayment and discharge of your loan over the property. Just before the settlement, you should sign the disposition and make arrangements to hand over the keys.

A new system of registration, known as Automated Registration of Title to Land, is gradually being introduced. This allows for electronic registration of land and property that is already registered in the Land Register If your sale is being done in this way, you will be asked to sign a mandate authorising your solicitor to sign the disposition electronically on your behalf.

After the settlement, your solicitor will settle your mortgage account and pay the balance to you after deducting his or her fees and expenses, or put the balance towards the purchase of your new home if you are also buying.

Information on conveyancing fees is given under costs in 5.8. When you are selling, the fees should cover:

- preliminary work, including exchanging missives, leading up to the conclusion of the bargain;

- conveyancing;

- handling the legal work connected with the discharge of the loan.

While this is being done, there are a number of things for you to attend to. They are described below and in Part 8.

Insurance and maintenance

Although the risk of loss or damage to the property passes to the buyer when missives are concluded, you should keep your own building and contents insurance in force until the date of entry, because you are responsible for maintaining the property until then. Sometimes the buyer will ask to visit the home before the date of entry, perhaps to measure up for curtains. While this is perfectly all right, it would not be a good idea to allow the buyer to do any significant work on the home before the date of entry, such as installing a cooker. There is always a chance that something may go wrong. Make sure that you tell your solicitor if you arrange for any repairs or find out about any local authority notices that affect the property and were not mentioned in your property questionnaire.

Outstanding costs

If you live in a flat and you are liable for any costs incurred as a result of a decision made under the terms of your title deeds or the Tenement Management Scheme, you will remain liable if the work or maintenance is arranged or carried out before the date your flat changes hands. However, before you sell, you, your fellow owners or your property manager can register a notice in the Land Register of Scotland or the Register of Sasines, depending on where your title deeds are registered, that you are potentially liable for unpaid costs. If a notice is registered at least 14 days before the date that the new owner acquires ownership, then your liability will be shared with the new owner (see *Common Repair, Common Sense* at 3.14).

Hire purchase, credit agreements and loans

Your contract with the buyer will normally require that there are no hire purchase or credit agreements or home improvement loans outstanding on any items included in the sale on the date of entry. Make sure that any of these are paid before the date of entry.

Periodic charges and outgoings

If you are paying any property management charges, you should give your solicitor details of these so that they can be apportioned at the date of entry. You should also make sure that he or she has details of your council tax banding and pays all outstanding charges until the date of entry.

Settlement

At settlement, a disposition (the document transferring the ownership or title from you to the buyer) in favour of the buyer is exchanged for the buyer's solicitor's cheque for the full purchase price. Your solicitor will pay any outstanding loans on the property from the sale proceeds, take off his or her fees and outgoings, and either give you a cheque for what is left, or put this towards the purchase price for your new home. You should also be given a detailed statement of all the transactions. Normally, you will receive the statement and any cheque on the day the sale is completed or very shortly afterwards.

The keys

Arrange with your solicitor to hand over the keys to the buyer. You can either deliver them to your solicitor on the date of entry or ask him or her to contact you and tell you when you can hand them over. **Never** hand over the keys before this.

7.7. Complaints

If you have a complaint about the chartered surveyor who carried out the survey and provided the valuation for your Home Report, see 4.3.

If you are unhappy with your solicitor's services, you should first try to sort things out directly with the solicitor. If you are unable to resolve the matter, complaints about solicitors are dealt with by the Scottish Legal Complaints Commission and the Law Society of Scotland – see 5.9.

All estate agents are required to belong to an estate agents' redress scheme approved by the Office of Fair Trading. The approved schemes are The Property Ombudsman and the Surveyors Ombudsman Service.

If you are unhappy with your estate agent's services, you should first try to sort things out directly with the estate agent. If you are still not happy, you can complain to whichever redress scheme the agent belongs to – The Property Ombudsman or the Surveyors Ombudsman Service. If the agent is a member of the National Association of Estate Agents, you can also complain to the association, which has powers to discipline its members.

If you believe there has been a breach of the Estate Agents Act or the Property Misdescriptions Act (see 3.5), you should contact your local trading standards department. For guidance on these Acts, see 7.8.

The Property Ombudsman

If you are unable to resolve a complaint with an estate agent, you should find out if the agent is a member of The Property Ombudsman scheme or the Surveyors Ombudsman Service.

The Property Ombudsman (see 7.8) will attempt to resolve complaints against members of the scheme by mediation or conciliation. If that fails and the ombudsman supports your complaint, the ombudsman has the power to award you compensation up to £25,000, which is binding on the agent.

Surveyors Ombudsman Service

Details of the Surveyors Ombudsman Service are given at 4.3, and contact details are at 4.4.

National Association of Estate Agents members

Estate agents who are members of the National Association of Estate Agents have the letters ANAEA, MNAEA or FMAEA after their names and the NAEA logo on their premises and stationery. Members of the association are required to comply with the Rules of Conduct and Code of Practice for Residential Estate Agency, which includes having an internal complaints procedure and a designated senior member of staff to deal with complaints.

If you have a complaint about an estate agent, you should first complain to the agent to attempt to resolve the problem. If you are unable to resolve your complaint, you should complain to the NAEA compliance officer (see 7.8). The association will look into all complaints providing there is no alternative means of resolving them. The association will not deal with complaints involving:

- Money outstanding or compensation, which you can take to the small claims court. You should get independent legal advice from a citizens' advice bureau or a solicitor before doing so.

- Allegations of a breach of the Estate Agents Act 1979 or the Property Misdescriptions Act 1991, which you should refer to the trading standards department of your local council.

- Matters on which legal proceedings have been started until the proceedings have been concluded.

- Conduct that occurred more than two years before you complained.

The association can discipline members found to be in breach of the rules of conduct and code of practice by a caution or formal warning. Members can also be brought before a disciplinary tribunal, which has the power to fine them for each breach of the rules, or to suspend or expel them from membership.

7.8. Further information

More information about the Home Report is available on the Scottish Government Home Report website: http://www. homereportscotland.gov.uk

A directory of chartered surveyors in Scotland and guides to understanding property surveys, and home buying and selling are available free of charge from the Royal Institution of Chartered Surveyors contact centre: tel: 0870 333 1600, e-mail: contactrics@rics.org. Ask for information on services in Scotland. You can also get informal advice from the professional information team at the contact centre. RICS Scotland has produced *Home Report: a guide for buyers and sellers in Scotland*, which is available from the contact centre or can be downloaded from www.rics.org/homereport

To make a complaint about a member of The Property Ombudsman scheme, contact The Property Ombudsman, Beckett House, 4 Bridge Street, Salisbury, Wiltshire SP1 2LX (tel: 01722 333306, e-mail: admin@tpos.co.uk). You can find information about the scheme and a list of members at http://www.tpos.co.uk/make_complaint_sales.htm

The National Association of Estate Agents can be contacted at: Arbon House, 6 Tournament Court, Edgehill Drive, Warwick CV34 6LG (tel: 01926 496800, e-mail: info@naea. co.uk) or visit the NAEA website http://www.naea.co.uk/ to find local members. To make a complaint about a member, contact the Compliance Officer at the above address, or e-mail: compliance@naea.co.uk

You can find guidance on the Estate Agents Act on the Office of Fair Trading website at: http://www.oft.gov.uk/shared_oft/business_leaflets/general/oft031.pdf and guidance on the Property Misdescriptions Act on the Department of Business, Enterprise and Regulatory Reform's website at: http://www.berr.gov.uk/files/file25449.pdf

Part 8

Organising the move

8.1. Doing it yourself or using a removal company

Doing your own move with the help of family or friends is a lot less expensive than using a removal company. Whether it is practical for you to do-it-yourself will depend on:

• the amount of furniture and other possessions you have;

• whether you can handle large or awkward items of furniture;

• the ease of exit from your current home and entry to your new home;

• the availability of willing and able helpers;

• whether you are fit and strong enough;

• how well you can cope with what for many people is a very stressful experience;

• whether you have other commitments, for example, children or work, which cut down the time you have available to get organised;

• the distance involved.

The basic cost of doing-it-yourself is the van hire charge, insurance to cover the move and petrol, or insurance and petrol alone if you can borrow a van from a friend or your employer. Before you hire or borrow a van, be sure that you can cope with driving it and that it is big enough to avoid making too many trips. There is a limit of 7.5 tonnes laden weight to a van you can drive with an ordinary licence from the age of 18. Hire firms can set their own minimum age limits above this and will usually require you to have held a full, clean licence for at least one year.

The more you have to move and the further the distance, the more sense it makes to use a removal company. Also bear in mind that if your doing-it-yourself move runs late, you may incur claims against you by your buyer and his or her removal company.

8.2. Finding a remover and getting a quotation

Get a quotation from two or three removal companies. If you have used a removal company before and were happy with its service, ask it to give you a quote. You can find other companies through personal recommendation, in the *Yellow Pages* or on the Internet. The British Association of Removers (BAR) is the trade organisation that represents most leading removal and storage companies. For the names of some of its local members, contact the BAR (see 8.8). A smaller trade organisation is the National Guild of Removers and Storers (NGRS). For the names of some of its local members, contact the NGRS (see 8.8).

When the estimators come round, remember to show them what you have to move in the garage, garden and loft, as well as your home contents. Decide whether to do your own packing or to ask the removers to do this, so that you can compare quotes. Assess the value of the contents of your home, what needs special attention (such as certain pieces of furniture or clothes) and discuss this with the estimator. Packing some items yourself may save you some money but the removers will not accept responsibility for items they did not pack.

If you want to put your home contents into store, most removal companies will charge a weekly rate according to the volume, with a minimum storage charge of four weeks. Make sure you ask the contractor for 'keep forward' labels to attach to any items you may want in advance of complete clearance.

Removers will unpack for you, if this was included in the quotation. This could be important if you work full-time, are elderly, unfit or have small children, and the remover's insurance policy will almost certainly require that the insured goods are unpacked by the professional remover. However, it will be more expensive and you will need to decide in advance where everything is to go, although you can arrange for unpacked items to be placed on flat surfaces ready for you to put away later.

Most removal companies will sell you packaging materials and will lend you cartons for linen, pictures/mirrors, books and china, and temporary wardrobes for clothes.

You are responsible for arranging the disconnection of electric light fittings, appliances and mains services such as gas and telephone. It is also your responsibility to tell the remover about access to your new home, for example, whether there is a lift, problems with parking, a long driveway or narrow staircases to be negotiated.

Removal costs take account of the time taken, the distance to be travelled and the volume of your possessions. A company may charge you more if you have possessions that are particularly heavy or difficult to move, for example, a piano or large, heavy wardrobe. Quotations for your removal will vary according to the companies' workloads, the time of year and day of the week. Fridays and the beginning and end of the month are always the busiest times. Choosing a different day of the week and time of the month could save you as much as 20 per cent.

The lowest quotation is not necessarily the best. You are moving the entire contents of your home, so check carefully what is included and what is excluded in the services offered.

8.3. Insurance

If you have a home contents insurance policy, it may cover your possessions during a move. If not, you may be able to get a temporary extension, for an additional premium. An insurance company is unlikely to offer you insurance for a move if you do not already have a policy with it. Most removal companies and all BAR and NGRS members provide a minimum level of insurance. BAR members are bound by BAR's liability terms, which require that they are insured. Once you have declared the total value of your goods, the remover accepts liability for them. Normally, liability is set at £25,000, although you can increase the value at an additional cost.

Whether you rely on your own insurance or the remover's insurance, check that the cover offered is appropriate and adequate and make a note of the time limit for claims. Don't forget that the remover's insurance will not cover items you pack yourself. If you rely on your own home contents insurance for cover, it may also exclude items you pack yourself. Check with your insurance company.

8.4. Planning your move

Plan ahead. There is a checklist at 8.6, which includes the information below.

The date. Arrange this as far ahead as possible. Cancellation or postponement can be costly.

Your new home. A map showing your new address and a contact telephone number will be helpful for the removal company, friends and relatives.

Whom to tell. Besides friends and relatives, many other people have an interest in your whereabouts. You will find some of them in the checklist in 8.6. If you have lots of people to tell, it might be worthwhile have change-of-address cards printed or sending e-mails, giving your new address, telephone number and the date you will be moving.

Mains services. Your remover is not allowed to disconnect mains services. Make arrangements with your energy supplier well in advance to disconnect the cooker if you are taking it with you, and check that any other appliances can be easily disconnected on moving day. On the day, phone your energy supplier and give it a final reading, or you may be held responsible for power and fuel used until the next reading.

Telephone. Contact the telephone company providing the service to your new home and arrange to take over the service from the date of entry. If necessary, inform your Internet service provider.

Deep freezer. Run down food stocks. Your remover will not accept responsibility for the contents.

Carpets and curtains. Check your quotation. Usually your remover will take down curtains and blinds and lift carpets if you ask for this to be included. They will not put them up again or re-lay fitted carpets.

System furniture. This can be a problem. Although designed to be dismantled and reassembled, in practice it may not reassemble so well. This type of problem cannot be covered by insurance.

Packing. How much the remover does depends on what you asked it to quote for. If you are paying for a complete service, leave it to them.

Insurance. See 8.3.

Special items. If you are concerned about items such as plants, IT equipment, antiques, fine art or a wine collection, discuss these is advance with your remover.

Don't take what you don't need. Treat your move as an opportunity for a ruthless sort out of unwanted possessions. Local charity shops welcome china, glass, books, ornaments, jewellery, pictures and good quality clothing, and some charitable organisations will take unwanted furniture and appliances to give to people who need them. Local volunteers will uplift cartons and sacks. If you have unwanted possessions that are not worth passing on, you should think about hiring a skip to dump them in, rather than leaving the new owner to deal with them.

8.4.1. Moving out and in on the same day

Moving day can be very stressful, the more so if you are selling your home and buying another, as most such transactions are arranged to take place on the same day. You should make sure that you are clear about the timing of arrangements for the exchange of payments for both the sale and the purchase, the exchange of keys and your remover's arrival and departure, especially if you are moving to another part of the country.

8.5. Just before moving day

The following preparations will help you and your remover whether you are packing yourself or the remover is doing it for you.

China and glassware. Have crockery and glassware ready on a level surface for packing.

Drawers. Leave clothes and other light items in drawers but do not lock or over-fill them. Heavier items, such as books and tools, should be removed and packed separately.

Plan where things are going to go. Work out where you want your possessions to go in your new home. It will be helpful to draw a plan, give a copy to the remover's supervisor and make sure that someone will be there to show where things are to go. Write the names of the rooms on the plan and prepare labels for these rooms to go on boxes and furniture.

Make a note of what goes into boxes. As boxes are packed, label them with a description of their contents.

Parking. Warn your remover if there are any restrictions outside your new home. One removal van needs about 15 metres of parking space. It helps if the van can be parked close to the property.

Flats. If you are moving into a block of flats with a lift, you will need to arrange priority. If the lift is small or there isn't one, warn the removers in advance.

Unloading. Warn your removers about any hazards such as poor access, small doorways, and spiral staircases.

Spare key. If possible, give the supervisor a spare key, in case the van arrives before you do.

Children and pets. Try to arrange for friends or neighbours to look after young children or pets or both on the removal day.

Payment. Check the quotation for the removal firm's terms of payment. They may want payment in advance or a cheque or even cash on the removal day. BAR members offer a Prepayment Guarantee. Ask the firm for details.

Important and valuable items. Gather together in one place the things you may need on the day of the move, such as keys, phone, cheque book, cash, map, telephone numbers of your solicitor and the removal firm, and so on.

The following preparations will be helpful to the new owner of your home:

- Look out instruction books and guarantees, and so on.

- Write out basic instructions about how to operate the central heating, security system, and so on.

- Pin up, in a prominent place, details of your new address and telephone number so that the new owner can contact you or pass them on to others trying to contact you.

8.6. Your responsibilities – a checklist of things that need to be done

The following checklist should be photocopied and pinned in a prominent place.

- Confirm dates with remover

- Sign and return contract, with payment if required in advance

- Arrange insurance

- Arrange contact telephone number

- Dispose of unwanted possessions

- Start running down freezer contents

- Contact carpet fitters if needed

- Book mains services disconnections

- Take final meter readings

- Notify doctor, dentist, optician and vet

- Notify bank, building society, investment accounts

- Notify tax office

- Arrange final telephone bill and the takeover of service in new home
- Notify internet service provider
- Arrange Royal Mail redirection
- Notify TV licensing and vehicle registration authorities
- Notify HP and credit firms
- Make local map for friends and remover
- Clear loft
- Organise parking at new home
- Plan where things are to go in new home
- Cancel milk and newspapers
- Clean out freezer
- Arrange minders for children and pets
- Find and label keys
- Gather together instructions for new owner
- Pin up details of new address and telephone number
- Send new address details to friends and relatives
- Separate trinkets, jewellery and small items
- Sort out linen and clothes
- Put garage/garden tools together
- Take down curtains and blinds
- Take down light fittings
- Collect children's toys
- Put together basic catering, including a kettle, for new home
- Put aside box or bag for important and valuable items

8.7. What to do if things go wrong

Things can and sometimes do go wrong in a complex operation such as moving home. You should at the least have adequate insurance cover. If you notice any breakages or damage before the removers leave, point them out to the supervisor, write the details on your contract and get him or her to initial them. Any of your possessions that are damaged or broken during the move should be kept for inspection by the company, or your insurers if you claim on the insurance policy. Make sure you claim within any specified time limit.

BAR members are covered by a code or practice approved by the Office of Fair Trading, which says that if the removal company were to cancel a removal more than ten days before the agreed date for the work, it must refund any money the customer has already paid. If it cancels less than ten days before the agreed date it must refund 150% of the money paid.

If you have a complaint about a removal company, write to it setting out your complaint and tell it what you expect it to do about it. If you are not satisfied with its response and the company is a member of the BAR, write to the BAR's Consumer Affairs Manager (see 8.8). The BAR has conciliation and arbitration services to help resolve disputes with its members.

BAR conciliation and arbitration schemes

To use the conciliation scheme, write to the BAR giving details of your dispute. The BAR will give details to the removal firm and ask for a response within 14 days. The BAR will then suggest a solution. If neither party accepts it, the matter can be referred to an arbitration scheme operated by the Chartered Institute of Arbitrators, independently of the BAR.

Under the arbitration scheme, you can claim for poor service but you cannot claim compensation for any amount more than £5,000, nor for physical injury or illness or the consequences of such injury or illness.

NGRS conciliation and ombudsman schemes

If you are not satisfied with the response to a complaint about a NGRS member, write to the NGRS Customer Services Department (see 8.8) giving details of your dispute. The NGRS will respond to you within ten days, give details to the removal firm and ask for a response. The NGRS will then suggest a solution, normally within two weeks. If neither party accepts it, the matter can be referred to the Removals Industry Ombudsman Scheme.

If you have a dispute that lies outwith the BAR conciliation and arbitration schemes or the Removals Industry Ombudsman Scheme, or if it is with a removal company that is not a BAR or NGRS member, you should get legal advice.

8.8. Further information

For information about the services of the British Association of Removers, details of local BAR members or to make a complaint about a member, contact the British Association of Removers, Tangent House, 62 Exchange Road, Watford WD18 0TG (tel: **01923 699480**, e-mail: info@bar.co.uk, http://www.bar.co.uk). You can download the guides:
Avoid the headache – a guide to a successful move from http://www.bar.co.uk/Move_With_BAR/Moving_Home_UK_Europe.aspx
Storage – the practical solution from http://www.bar.co.uk/Move_With_BAR/Storage.aspx

For information about the National Guild of Removers and Storers, details of local NGRS members or to make a complaint about a member, contact the National Guild of Removers and Storers, PO Box 690, Chesham, Buckinghamshire HP5 1WR (tel: 01494 792279, e-mail: info@ngrs.co.uk, http://www.ngrs.co.uk/).

Index

Note: Page numbers in **bold** indicate **major topics.**